◪SCHOLASTIC

100 LITERACY ASSESSMENT LESSONS

TERMS AND CONDITIONS

IMPORTANT - PERMITTED USE AND WARNINGS - READ CAREFULLY BEFORE USING

Licence

YEAR 5

Scottish Primary 6

Minimum specification:
- PC or Mac with a CD-ROM drive and 512 Mb RAM (recommended)
- Windows 2000 or above/Mac OSX version 10.4 or above
- Recommended minimum processor speed: 1 GHz

For all technical support queries, please phone Scholastic Customer Services on 0845 603 9091.

Gillian Howell

CREDITS

Author
Gillian Howell

Editors
Michael Ward and
Linda Mellor

Series Designers
Joy Monkhouse and
Melissa Leeke

Designers
Sonja Bagley, Andrea Lewis,
Allison Parry and
Quadrum Ltd

Illustrations
Simon Smith/Beehive
Illustration (unless
otherwise credited)

CD-ROM development
CD-ROM developed
in association with
Vivid Interactive

ACKNOWLEDGEMENTS

The publishers gratefully acknowledge permission to reproduce the following copyright material: **Clare Bevan** for the use of 'The Music Lesson Rap' by Clare Bevan from *The Rhyme Riot* by Clare Bevan © 2002, Clare Bevan (2002, Macmillan Children's Books). **David Higham Associates** for the use of an extract from *The Impractical Chimney-Sweep* by Rosemary Anne Sisson © 1956, Rosemary Anne Sisson (1956, Macmillan) and for the electronic use of an extract from *Alone on a Wide, Wide Sea* by Michael Morpurgo © 2006, Michael Morpurgo (2006, HarperCollins). **Jan Dean** for the use of 'An Owl Flew in my Bedroom Once' by Jan Dean from *A Mean Fish Smile* by Roger Stevens, Sue Cowling and Jan Dean © 2000, Jan Dean (2000, Macmillan Children's Books). **Aidan Gibbons** for the use of the film *The Piano* by Aidan Gibbons © 2007, Aidan Gibbons (2007, Aidan Gibbons). **HarperCollins** for the print use of extracts from *Alone on a Wide Wide Sea* by Michael Morpurgo © 2006, Michael Morpurgo (2006, HarperCollins). **Brian Moses** for the use of 'The Lost Angels' by Brian Moses from *Behind the Staffroom Door: The Very Best of Brian Moses* by Brian Moses © 1998, Brian Moses (2007, Macmillan Children's Books).

Every effort has been made to trace copyright holders for the works reproduced in this book, and the publishers apologise for any inadvertent omissions.

Text © 2009, Gillian Howell
© 2009, Scholastic Ltd

Designed using Adobe
InDesign

Published by Scholastic Ltd
Villiers House
Clarendon Avenue
Leamington Spa
Warwickshire CV32 5PR

Visit our website at
www.scholastic.co.uk

Printed by Bell and Bain Ltd

Mixed Sources
Product group from well-managed
forests and other controlled sources
www.fsc.org Cert no. TT-COC-002769
© 1996 Forest Stewardship Council

British Library Cataloguing-in-Publication Data
A catalogue record for this book is available from the British Library.
ISBN 978-1407-10187-3
The right of Gillian Howell to be identified as the author of this work has been asserted by her in accordance with the Copyright, Designs and Patents Act 1988.

Contents

100 Literacy Assessment Lessons: Year 5

'Assessment' refers to all those activities undertaken by teachers, and by their students in assessing themselves, which provide information to be used as feedback to modify the teaching and learning activities in which they are engaged.'

from Black and William *Inside the Black Box*

About the series

100 Literacy Assessment Lessons is a response to the Assessment for Learning strategy (AfL) and Assessing Pupils' Progress (APP) and contains all new, stand-alone material. The lessons mirror the guidelines and viewpoints of the revised approach to assessment. The CD-ROMs provide appropriate and exciting texts and a variety of assessment activities from photocopiable pages for individual, whole-class or group work to stimulating interactive activities. Together, the books and CD-ROMs will be an invaluable resource to help you understand and implement the revised approach to assessment.

About assessment

The key points of the revised approach to assessment are as follows:
- Assessments are accurate and linked to National Curriculum levels;
- Assessments are targeted, with assessment focuses used as the guiding criteria;
- Assessments are reliable and based on a range of evidence;
- Assessments are useful and appropriate: day to day, periodic or transitional.

Type of assessment	Purpose	Strategies
Day to day	Ongoing and formative: encourages reflection and informs the next steps in teaching and learning.	Objectives, outcomes and success criteria are made explicit and are shared with children; observations are used to gather evidence; peer assessment and self-assessment help to develop children as responsible learners.
Periodic	Provides a periodic view of children's progress and diagnostic information linked to national standards.	Progress and attainment are reviewed regularly (half-termly or termly) against APP criteria; strengths and gaps in learning are identified to inform future planning.
Transitional	Brings together evidence, including tests, at points of transition (eg level to level or year to year); provides a formal overview of children's attainment set within the framework of national standards.	Use of formal tasks and tests; external validation and reporting.

For a complete list of strategies for day-to-day assessment and further information about periodic and transitional assessment, visit the National Strategies website (**http://nationalstrategies.standards.dcsf.gov.uk**).

What are assessment focuses (AFs)?

Assessment focuses (AFs) are tools for assessment that sit between the National Curriculum programmes of study and level descriptions. The AFs provide more detailed criteria against which children's standards of attainment can be assessed and judged.

About the book

Reflecting the structure of the renewed Primary Framework for Literacy (2006), the book is divided into three Blocks: Narrative, Non-fiction and Poetry. Each Block is further divided into Units, and the Units are split into Phases. The Phases are divided into a number of day-to-day assessment activities. These assessment activities, based on learning outcomes, are designed to fit easily into your existing planning.

Units

Each Unit covers a different text-type or genre and, because of this, each Unit has its own introduction containing the following:

Literacy objectives: All objectives for the Unit are listed under their strand names.

Key aspects of learning: Aspects of learning that the Unit covers are identified from the renewed Primary National Strategy (PNS) Framework.

Assessment focuses (AFs): The main assessment focuses that are addressed during the Unit are listed from APP.

Speaking and listening: Assessment areas you should look out for are linked to the speaking and listening strand objectives.

Resources: Lists all of the resources required for the activities in each Phase.

Planning grids: There are two grids per Unit to provide an overview of the Unit and to suggest how you can build assessment opportunities into your medium-term planning. The grids show Phases, learning outcomes, a summary of lessons, assessment opportunities and potential evidence, levelled statements of the assessment focuses (AFs) and success criteria matched to the learning outcomes in the form of 'I can...' statements.

Assessment activities

Each assessment activity follows the same format:

Learning outcomes: These are relevant to individual activities or a set of activities that share objectives.

Success criteria: These are child-friendly 'I can...' statements for children or teachers to refer to during or following the activity.

Setting the context: This section provides guidance on what the task is and details the children's expected prior learning. The context for the task may also be explained: group, paired or individual work. Where adult support is required, this is also described.

Assessment opportunity: This section highlights what to assess, how to find out what children know, and what questions to ask.

Assessment evidence: This section suggests what to look for during an activity in relation to specific assessment focuses (AFs).

Next steps: This section is divided into support and extension. It provides ideas to enable children to revisit an objective or learning outcome, and gives feedback or targets to move children forward, consolidate or extend their learning.

Key aspects of learning: Key aspects of learning are linked to specific activities.

Photocopiable pages

At the end of each Unit is a selection of photocopiable activity pages. The full range of these is provided on the CD-ROM, including levelled versions where appropriate. Photocopiable pages may include self-assessment statements for ticking as well as a 'traffic light' system for colouring (see 'Self-assessment' on page 7 for more information.) Where 'I can...' statements are not included, peer assessment may be suggested within an activity.

Transitional assessment

Also included on the CD-ROM are some SATs-style formal single-level assessments. More information about these can be found on page 7, and a grid detailing their content is provided on page 174.

How to use the materials

The activities in the book provide a balance of whole-class/group/paired/ independent learning and teaching, and give the opportunity not only for day-to-day assessment but also for collection of evidence against individual assessment focuses (AFs) for periodic review. Each activity can be slotted into a lesson where appropriate and may involve discussion work, written responses, use of photocopiable pages or interactive activities.

Two periodic assessment activities are provided at the end of each Unit – one for reading and one for writing. The focus of each of these activities is usually a photocopiable page that assesses children on the learning outcomes covered during the Unit and provides further evidence against the assessment focuses. You can also use these periodic assessments to help you to make level judgements that match to the Reading and Writing Attainment Targets (ATs).

Making a level judgement

Assessment involves making a level judgement against national standards at regular intervals. The following steps will support you in adopting a strategic approach to the marking and levelling needed for assessment.

Step one: Consider evidence
- Use a range of appropriate evidence to make a level judgement, for example, written or oral;
- Remember that it is quality not quantity that matters;
- Keep examples of children's work that will provide significant evidence.

Step two: Review the evidence
- Take a broader view of a child's achievement across the whole subject and over time;
- Create a visual picture of strengths and learning gaps by highlighting criteria a child has met across a range of evidence;
- Collaborate with colleagues and agree what constitutes success for the various assessment criteria.

Step three: Make a judgement
- Consult the English Assessment Guidelines (see National Standards website: **http://nationalstrategies.standards.dcsf.gov.uk**) and look at exemplar material provided in the Standards files;
- Arrive at an overall subject level judgement;
- Think about what the child demonstrates:
  - How much of the level;
  - How consistently;
  - How independently;
  - In what range of contexts.
- Finally, fine-tune your levelling to 'high', 'secure' or 'low'.

What's on the CD-ROM?

Each CD-ROM contains a wealth of resources. These include:
- **Photocopiable pages:** levelled where appropriate, including text extracts and activity sheets for day-to-day and periodic assessment.
- **Transitional assessments:** single-level tests for levels 2–5 including mark schemes and instructions.
- **Interactive activities:** for individuals or small groups, with in-built marking to assess specific learning outcomes.
- **Whiteboard tools:** a set of tools (including a pen, highlighter, eraser, notes and reward stickers) that can be used to annotate activity sheets or interactive activities. These tools will work on any interactive whiteboard or conventional screen.
- **Editable planning grids** (in Word format) are available to help teachers integrate the assessment activities into their medium-term and weekly planning.

How to use the CD-ROM

System requirements
Minimum specification:
- PC or Mac with a CD-ROM drive and 512 Mb RAM (recommended)
- Windows 2000 or above/Mac OSX version 10.4 or above
- Recommended minimum processor speed: 1 GHz

Getting started
The *100 Literacy Assessment Lessons* CD-ROM should auto run when inserted into your CD drive. If it does not, browse to your CD drive to view the contents of the CD-ROM and click on the *100 Literacy Assessment Lessons* icon.

From the start-up screen you will find four options: select **Credits** to view a list of acknowledgements. Click on **Register** to register the product in order to receive product updates and special offers. Click on **How to use this CD-ROM** to access support notes for using the CD-ROM. Finally, if you agree to the terms and conditions, select **Start** to move to the main menu.

For all technical support queries, contact Scholastic Customer Services help desk on 0845 603 9091.

Navigating the CD-ROM
The CD-ROM allows users to search for resources by Block or Unit, or by assessment focus. Users can also search by assessment type (day to day, periodic or transitional) or by resource type (for example, worksheet, interactive resource, or text extract).

Day-to-day assessments
These should be used to support learning. They can be used during a lesson, when you judge that children are ready for an assessment activity. The materials can also be used weekly or after a unit of work has been completed.

Periodic assessments
These can be used with a group of children rather than with the whole class. This could be at the end of a unit of work (for example, at the end of a half-term or term). Decide who is ready to be assessed using the outcomes of the day-to-day assessment activities and your observations of children's performance.

Self-assessment
There is a 'traffic light' system at the bottom of some photocopiable pages that children can shade to show how they feel about the activity: red for 'need help'; orange for 'have some understanding'; green for 'I found this easy!'. (Alternatively, you may wish to utilise these as a teacher marking tool for providing an at-a-glance guide to the child's progress.)

The photocopiable sheets also provide 'I can...' statements with tick boxes, to enable children to self-assess specifically in terms of the relevant learning outcomes/success criteria. A similar system is in place at the end of all the interactive activities, where the children are asked to click on a traffic light, and to type in any comments.

Transitional tests
These single-level tests provide evidence of where, in relation to national standards, children are at a given point in time. There are two Reading and Writing assessments for each level. Each Reading assessment consists of a two-part reading comprehension test based on two different text types. Each Writing assessment consists of two writing tasks - shorter and longer - that focus on writing for different purposes. All the tasks and tests for levels 2-5 are included on the CD-ROM together with easy-to-follow marking schemes (see pages 174-175 for more information).

Class PET
A whole-school version of *100 Literacy Assessment Lessons* is available with an expanded range of digital assessment activities, as well as the facility to report, record and track children's work. For further information visit the Class PET website, **www.scholastic.co.uk/classpet**.

Periodic assessment

Unit	AT	Page	Assessment focuses	Learning outcomes
Narrative 1	Reading	22	AF2, AF5, AF6	Children can express their opinion of a story with reference to other work by the same author. Children can talk about the distinctive features of an author's style by referring to characters, themes, settings or use of language.
	Writing	23	AF3	Children can write a complete story with a sequence of events arranged into paragraphs, linked with a range of connectives and varying sentence length.
Narrative 2	Reading	43	AF4, AF7	Children can identify the different features of traditional stories, myths and legends.
	Writing	43	AF1	Children can write a new version of a myth or legend, identifying their audience and adapting their writing to suit this audience. Children can reflect critically on their own writing and edit and improve it.
Narrative 3	Reading	59	AF2, AF6, AF7	Children can highlight similarities and differences between characters. Children can identify and explain key phrases. Children can reflect on reading habits and explore preferences.
	Writing	59	AF1	Children can edit and improve their writing. Children can use features of stories from other cultures, different authorial voices and reported speech in their own writing.
Narrative 4	Reading	69	AF2, AF5, AF6, AF7	Children can understand how characters are introduced. Children can identify aspects of writing that vary between formal and informal.
	Writing	70	AF1–AF8	Children can draft an historical newspaper report.
Narrative 5	Reading	81	AF2, AF6	Children can identify different ways to engage and interrogate text to deepen their understanding. Children can identify backgrounds of characters.
	Writing	82	AF1, AF2, AF6, AF8	Children can reflect critically on their own writing and edit and improve it.
Narrative 6	Reading	96	AF4, AF5	Children can identify differences between written playscripts and news scripts. Children can identify language features of news.
	Writing	96	AF2	Children can evaluate their own work in writing and analysing different types of script.

Unit	AT	Page	Assessment focuses	Learning outcomes
Non-fiction 1	Reading	108	AF4, AF5	Children demonstrate that they can evaluate sets of instructions (including attempting to follow some of them) for purpose, organisation and layout, clarity and usefulness.
	Writing	109	AF3	Children demonstrate that they can write an instructional text using appropriate form and features and awareness of intended audience. Children can reflect on their writing and edit and improve it, showing a clear understanding of the features of instructional writing.
Non-fiction 2	Reading	126	AF4, AF5	Children can identify the features of the most successful recount text. Children can understand the differences between the punctuation of reported and direct speech.
	Writing	126	AF3	Children can understand the differences between the punctuation of reported and direct speech. Children can use a variety of reporting clauses in dialogue and reported speech. Children can write a recount text using notes made from interviews.
Non-fiction 3	Reading	140	AF5, AF6	Children can understand features of a persuasive text. Children can understand how language is used for different purposes in persuasive texts.
	Writing	140	AF2, AF3, AF4	Children can develop a persuasive argument, using notes and feedback.
Poetry 1	Reading	150	AF4	Children can record and explain their understanding of the imagery in a poem. Children can identify similarities and differences in form and language features used. Children can understand the different structures used for different poems.
	Writing	151	AF3	Children can write a journal entry expressing preferences.
Poetry 2	Reading	164	AF4	Children understand the differences between literal and figurative language and can use the text to explain the effects of imagery in a poem.
	Writing	164	AF2	Children demonstrate that they are able to evaluate and improve their performance in the light of comments from others. Children can record their own evaluations of work and performance.
Poetry 3	Reading	171	AF5	Children can identify the key features of performance poetry. Children can apply varied tone-repeated patterns to a range of poems when performing.
	Writing	172	AF2, AF7	Children can write poems to reflect the identified techniques of performance poetry. Children can review their own learning and evaluate it against clear criteria.

NARRATIVE

UNIT 1 Significant authors

Literacy objectives

Speak and listen for a wide range of purposes in different contexts
Strand 3 Group discussion and interaction
- Plan and manage a group task over time using different levels of planning.
- Understand different ways to take the lead and support others in groups.
- Understand the process of decision making.

Read and write for a range of purposes on paper and on screen
Strand 7 Understanding and interpreting texts
- Infer writers' perspectives from what is written and from what is implied.
- Compare different types of narrative and information texts and identify how they are structured.
- Explore how writers use language for comic and dramatic effects.

Strand 8 Engaging with and responding to texts
- Reflect on reading habits and preferences and plan personal reading goals.
- Compare the usefulness of techniques, such as visualisation, prediction and empathy, in exploring the meaning of texts.

Strand 9 Creating and shaping texts
- Experiment with different narrative form and styles to write their own stories.

Strand 11 Sentence structure and punctuation
- Punctuate sentences accurately, including using speech marks and apostrophes.

Strand 12 Presentation
- Adapt handwriting for specific purposes, for example printing, use of italics.

Key aspects of learning

Evaluation
- As they read and compare the work of particular authors, children will express and justify their judgements about books and about the author's style.

Enquiry
- Children will decide how to answer questions about an author by using different sources of information, surveys of opinion and so on.

Social skills
- Children will participate in an extended group activity. They will take on a clearly defined role in the group, negotiate with others and reach agreement.

Self-awareness
- Children will discuss and reflect on their personal responses to the texts.

Communication
- Children will develop their ability to discuss as they work collaboratively in paired, group and whole-class contexts. They will communicate outcomes orally, in writing and through ICT if appropriate.

Assessment focuses

Reading
AF2 *(understand, describe, select or retrieve information, events or ideas from texts and use quotation and reference to text).*
AF3 *(deduce, infer or interpret information, events or ideas from texts).*
AF5 *(explain and comment on writers' use of language, including grammatical and literary features at word and sentence level).*
AF6 *(identify and comment on writers' purposes and viewpoints, and the overall effect of the text on the reader).*
AF7 *(relate texts to their social, cultural and historical contexts and literary traditions).*

Writing
AF5 *(vary sentences for clarity, purpose and effect).*
AF6 *(write with technical accuracy of syntax and punctuation in phrases, clauses and sentences).*

Speaking and listening
Group discussion and interaction (actively include and respond to all members of the group).

Resources

Phase 1 activities
Photocopiable page, 'Alone on a Wide Wide Sea (a)'
Photocopiable page, 'Begin at the beginning' (versions 1 and 2)
Photocopiable page, 'Alone on a Wide Wide Sea (b)'
Phase 2 activities
Interactive activity, 'Correctly written dialogue'
Phase 3 activities
Interactive activity, 'Identifying sentence types'
Photocopiable page, 'Top tips for giving a presentation' (versions 1 and 2)
Phase 4 activities
Photocopiable page, 'Tension' (versions 1 and 2)
Periodic assessment
Photocopiable page, 'Narrative 1 Reading assessment'
Recommended texts
Alone on a Wide Wide Sea by Michael Morpurgo (ISBN 978-0007-23056-3)
Kensuke's Kingdom by Michael Morpurgo (ISBN 978-1405-22174-0)
Someone's Watching, Someone's Waiting by Jamila Gavin (ISBN 978-0749-73106-9)
Heaven Eyes by David Almond (ISBN 978-0340-94497-4)

Unit 1 ☐ Significant authors

Learning outcomes	Assessment opportunity and evidence	Assessment focuses (AFs)		Success criteria
		Level 2	Level 3	
Phase ① activities pages 15–16				
Story opening in the first person Children can express their opinion of a story with reference to other work by the same author.	● Supported group activity where children read and analyse the opening of a story and compare it with stories by the same author. ● Children's oral and written responses on the photocopiable page. ● Notes made against the class list.	**Reading AF3** ● Simple, plausible inference about events and information, using evidence from text. ● Comments based on textual cues, sometimes misunderstood.	**Reading AF3** ● Straightforward inference based on a single point of reference in the text. ● Responses to text show meaning established at a literal level or based on personal speculation.	● I can compare different story openings by the same author, identifying similarities and differences.
Visualisation Children can visualise a setting and make predictions about events that might happen there.	● Small group activity where children read and explore a shared text and perform a role play. ● Children's role-play activity and oral responses.	**Reading AF3** ● Simple, plausible inference about events and information, using evidence from text. ● Comments based on textual cues, sometimes misunderstood.	**Reading AF3** ● Straightforward inference based on a single point of reference in the text. ● Responses to text show meaning established at a literal level.	● I can use visualisation to explore a text. ● I can empathise with a character and explain how they might feel in a particular setting.
Phase ② activity page 17				
Writing dialogue Children can write a new scene for a story in the style of the author. They can organise the scene into a sequence of paragraphs.	● Paired activity where children role play a conversation and write them as dialogue. ● Children's role-play and written outcomes.	**Writing AF6** ● Clause structure mostly grammatically correct. ● Sentence demarcation with capital letters and full stops usually accurate. ● Some accurate use of question and exclamation marks, and commas in lists.	**Writing AF6** ● Straightforward sentences usually demarcated accurately with full stops, capital letters, question and exclamation marks. ● Some, limited, use of speech punctuation. ● Comma splicing evident, particularly in narrative.	● I can write a new scene for a story in paragraphs. ● I can write dialogue accurately.
Phase ③ activities pages 18–19				
Improving sentences Children can vary sentences with different techniques to maintain interest.	● Independent activity where children identify and explain the differences between simple, compound and complex sentences. ● Children's oral responses and completed interactive activity.	**Reading AF5** ● Some effective language choices noted. ● Some familiar patterns of language identified.	**Reading AF5** ● A few basic features of writer's use of language identified, but with little or no comment.	● I can identify simple and compound sentences. ● I can identify complex sentences.
Presenting information Children can work effectively as part of a group to research a significant author and make a presentation to the class.	● Group activity where children make a presentation, and then assess it and write tips for effective presentations. ● Children's oral self-assessments, notes against the class list and written responses on the photocopiable page.	**Reading AF2** ● Some specific, straightforward information recalled. ● Generally clear idea of where to look for information. **Reading AF6** ● Some awareness that writers have viewpoints and purposes. ● Simple statements about likes and dislikes in reading, sometimes with reasons.	**Reading AF2** ● Simple, most obvious points identified though there may also be some misunderstanding. ● Some comments include quotations from or references to text, but not always relevant. **Reading AF6** ● Comments identify main purpose. ● Express personal response but with little awareness of writer's viewpoint or effect on reader.	● I can contribute to group research. ● I can deliver an oral presentation to the class.

Unit 1 Significant authors

Learning outcomes	Assessment opportunity and evidence	Assessment focuses (AFs)		Success criteria
		Level 2	Level 3	
Phase ④ activities pages 20–21				
Creating tension Children know narrative techniques for creating tension.	• Supported group activity where children identify techniques an author has used to create tension. • Group discussion. • Teacher observation and group written outcomes.	**Reading AF5** • Some effective language choices noted. • Some familiar patterns of language identified.	**Reading AF5** • A few basic features of writer's use of language identified, but with little or no comment.	I can identify how short sentences are used to create tension.
Writing a suspense paragraph Children can write their own paragraph applying knowledge from reading.	• Paired activity where children write a paragraph that conveys tension and evaluate a partner's writing. • Children's written paragraphs and paired evaluations.	**Writing AF5** • Some variation in sentence openings. • Mainly simple sentences with and used to connect clauses. • Past and present tense generally consistent.	**Writing AF5** • Reliance mainly on simple structured sentences, variation with support. • *and, but, so* are the most common connectives, subordination occasionally. • Some limited variation in use of tense and verb forms, not always secure.	I can write paragraphs using suspense.

Learning outcomes	Assessment opportunity and evidence	Assessment focuses (AFs)		Success criteria
		Level 4	Level 5	
Phase ① activities pages 15–16				
Story opening in the first person • Children know the features of a good story opening. • Children can express their opinion of a story with reference to other work by the same author.	• Independent activity where children read and analyse the opening of a story and compare it with stories by the same author. • Children's oral and written responses on the photocopiable page.	**Reading AF3** • Comments make inferences based on evidence from different points in the text. • Inferences often correct, but comments are not always rooted securely in the text or repeat narrative or content.	**Reading AF3** • Comments develop explanation of inferred meanings drawing on evidence across the text. • Comments make inferences and deductions based on textual evidence.	• I can identify how authors introduce characters and problems to a story. • I can compare different story openings by the same author, identifying similarities and differences.
Visualisation Children can visualise a setting and make predictions about events that might happen there.	• Small group activity where children read and explore a shared text and perform a role play. • Children's role-play activity and oral responses.	**Reading AF3** • Comments make inferences based on evidence from different points in the text. • Inferences often correct, but comments are not always rooted securely in the text or repeat narrative or content.	**Reading AF3** • Comments develop explanation of inferred meanings drawing on evidence across the text. • Comments make inferences and deductions based on textual evidence.	• I can use visualisation to explore a text. • I can empathise with a character and explain how they might feel in a particular setting.
Phase ② activity page 17				
Writing dialogue Children can write a new scene for a story in the style of the author. They can organise the scene into a sequence of paragraphs.	• Paired activity where children role play a conversation and write them as dialogue. • Children's role-play and written outcomes.	**Writing AF6** • Sentences demarcated accurately throughout the text, including question marks. • Speech marks to denote speech generally accurate, with some other speech punctuation. • Commas used in lists and occasionally to mark clauses, although not always accurately.	**Writing AF6** • Full range of punctuation used accurately to demarcate sentences, including speech punctuation. • Syntax and punctuation within the sentence generally accurate including commas to mark clauses, though some errors occur where ambitious structures are attempted.	• I can write a new scene for a story in paragraphs. • I can write dialogue accurately.

Unit 1 ◻ Significant authors

Learning outcomes	Assessment opportunity and evidence	Assessment focuses (AFs)		Success criteria
		Level 4	Level 5	
Phase ③ activities pages 18-19				
Improving sentences Children can vary sentences with different techniques to maintain interest.	• Independent activity where children identify and explain the differences between simple, compound and complex sentences. • Children's oral responses and completed interactive activity.	**Reading AF5** • Some basic features of writer's use of language identified. • Simple comments on writer's choices.	**Reading AF5** • Various features of writer's use of language identified, with some explanation. • Comments show some awareness of the effect of writer's language choices.	• I can identify simple and compound sentences. • I can identify complex sentences.
Presenting information Children can work effectively as part of a group to research a significant author and make a presentation to the class.	• Group activity where children make a presentation, and then assess it and write tips for effective presentations. • Children's oral self-assessments, notes against the class list and written outcomes.	**Reading AF2** • Some relevant points identified. • Comments supported by some generally relevant textual reference or quotation. **Reading AF6** • Main purpose identified. • Simple comments show some awareness of writer's viewpoint. • Simple comment on overall effect on reader.	**Reading AF2** • Most relevant points clearly identified, including those selected from different places in the text. • Comments generally supported by relevant textual reference or quotation, even when points made are not always accurate. **Reading AF6** • Main purpose clearly identified, often through general overview. • Viewpoint in texts clearly identified, with some, often limited, explanation. • General awareness of effect on the reader, with some, often limited, explanation.	• I can contribute to group research. • I can deliver an oral presentation to the class.
Phase ④ activities pages 20-21				
Creating tension Children know narrative techniques for creating tension.	• Group activity where children identify techniques an author has used to create tension. • Teacher observation, notes against the class list and group written outcomes.	**Reading AF5** • Some basic features of writer's use of language identified. • Simple comments on writer's choices.	**Reading AF5** • Various features of writer's use of language identified, with some explanation. • Comments show some awareness of the effect of writer's language choices.	I can identify how short sentences are used to create tension.
Writing a suspense paragraph Children can write own paragraph applying knowledge from reading.	• Paired activity where children write a paragraph that conveys tension and evaluate a partner's writing. • Children's written paragraphs and paired evaluations.	**Writing AF5** • Some variety in length, structure or subject of sentences. • Use of some subordinating connectives throughout the text. • Some variation, generally accurate, in tense and verb forms.	**Writing AF5** • A variety of sentence lengths, structures and subjects provides clarity and emphasis. • Wider range of connectives used to clarify relationship between ideas. • Some features of sentence structure used to build up detail or convey shades of meaning.	I can write paragraphs using suspense.

Phase ①	**Story opening in the first person**

Learning outcome
Children can express their opinion of a story with reference to other work by the same author.

Success criteria
I can compare different story openings by the same author, identifying similarities and differences.

Setting the context
This activity should be carried out once children have read more than one short story written by the same author and listened to the opening chapter of the class novel being read. Ensure children have had the opportunity to discuss how the author opens different stories and introduces characters, exploring dialogue and setting description. If possible, children should have read the opening chapter of a Michael Morpurgo story that is different from *Alone on a Wide Wide Sea,* for example, *Kensuke's Kingdom.* Provide children with copies of the photocopiable pages 'Alone on a Wide Wide Sea (a)' and 'Begin at the beginning' (versions 1 or 2). Children working at levels 2–3 can use version 1 of 'Begin at the beginning'. Ask the children to read the story opening for *Alone on a Wide Wide Sea* and answer the questions on the second photocopiable page. Display the success criteria in the classroom.

Assessment opportunity
Children working at levels 2–3 work in a supported group and discuss the extract before completing version 1 of 'Begin at the beginning'. Children working at levels 4–5 will work independently to read and answer the questions. This will provide an opportunity to make notes of their oral responses.

Assessment evidence
At levels 2–3, children will identify features such as the first-person narration, conversational tone and that the new character is the narrator's sister. At levels 4–5, children will make inferences about the narrator and the content of the story, such as 'He might find out about the key and find out who his parents are'. Notes made during the activity, the children's annotated story opening and written responses to some of the questions on the photocopiable page will provide evidence for Reading AF3 (see also Reading AF2, AF5 and AF7).

Next steps
Support: For those children who struggle to analyse story openings, provide several stories written by another author and ask them to identify which begin with setting description, dialogue or action.
Extension: Provide different stories by other authors and ask children to compare and contrast first-person story openings with third-person openings.

Key aspects of learning
Evaluation: As they read and compare the work of particular authors, children will express and justify their judgements about books and about the author's style.
Self-awareness: Children will discuss and reflect on their personal responses to the texts.
Communication: Children will develop their ability to discuss as they work collaboratively in paired, group and whole-class contexts. They will communicate outcomes orally, in writing and through ICT if appropriate.

NARRATIVE

Phase ① Visualisation

Learning outcome
Children can visualise a setting and make predictions about events that might happen there.

Success criteria
- I can use visualisation to explore a text.
- I can empathise with a character and explain how they might feel in a particular setting.

Setting the context
This activity should be undertaken once children have explored different settings and characters in stories written by the same author. They should have been given opportunities to empathise with characters and to explore how the setting affects the characters and the plots of stories. If you have not read *Alone on a Wide Wide Sea* to the class, set the scene by explaining that Arthur had travelled across the sea to Australia with a group of orphans and had a long journey across Australia to a place called Cooper's Station. Enlarge a copy of the photocopiable page 'Alone on a Wide Wide Sea (b)' and read the setting description to the children. Discuss the setting with the children. Invite them to close their eyes for a moment and 'see' the setting in their mind's eye. Ask them to say how they think they would feel, arriving after a long journey into an unknown place. Together, mark up details on the copy that describe the setting. Annotate the text to show the author's use of the senses. Ask them how the author gives clues about what it might be like for the children in this place. Ask the children in small groups to role play arriving at Cooper's Station. Allow them enough time to discuss and plan their role play before they enact it.

Assessment opportunity
Observe the children's role plays and make observational notes. When the children have finished their role plays, invite them to describe their responses, saying how they felt and why. Ask them what else they might have seen or heard in the setting. Make notes of their oral responses.

Assessment evidence
At levels 2-3, children will show their response to the setting by referring to direct evidence in the text, for example, 'I could hear cows and smell them'. At levels 4-5, children will show empathy with the characters by expressions of bewilderment, excitement, fear, or curiosity. Use children's role play and your notes on their oral responses to provide evidence for Reading AF3.

Next steps
Support: For children who struggled to visualise the setting, ask them to use the information in the text to draw a plan of Cooper's Station showing each of the physical features in the text - the huge sheds, the creek, the farmhouse and the animals.
Extension: Invite children to write a conversation between two characters when they go to bed that night to show how they feel about their new home and what they think the future will be like there.

Key aspects of learning
Social skills: Children will participate in an extended group activity. They will take on a clearly defined role in the group, negotiate with others and reach agreement.
Self-awareness: Children will discuss and reflect on their personal responses to the texts.
Communication: Children will develop their ability to discuss as they work collaboratively in paired, group and whole-class contexts. They will communicate outcomes orally, in writing and through ICT if appropriate.

Phase ② Writing dialogue

Learning outcomes
● Children can write a new scene for a story in the style of the author. They can organise the scene into a sequence of paragraphs.
● Children can write conversations using direct speech.

Success criteria
● I can write a new scene for a story in paragraphs.
● I can write dialogue accurately.

Setting the context
This activity should be carried out after the children have explored the use of dialogue in stories written by the same author and in the class novel. They should have revised the rules for writing, punctuating and laying out dialogue. Display the success criteria in the classroom. Ask the children to work with a partner. Ask one of the partners to take the role of a character from one of the stories they have been studying, and the other to be him or herself but in the story as a new character. Invite them to role play a conversation between the characters. When they have performed the role play, ask them to write their new conversations in a new scene for the story on paper or using a computer. Children working at levels 2–3 may write only three paragraphs.

Assessment opportunity
Observe children as they perform their role-play conversations and make notes of children's abilities to think in role and convey character through conversation. Children's written conversations can also be used to show their security in punctuating sentences and laying out dialogue on the page.

Assessment evidence
At levels 2–3, children will demonstrate use of simple dialogue with limited use of speech marks. Other forms of punctuation such as capital letters and full stops will usually be used accurately. At levels 4–5, children will use more complex sentence structures. Use children's role-play and written conversations to provide evidence for Writing AF6.

Next steps
Support: Children who demonstrate insecurity about punctuation and layout of dialogue can complete the interactive activity 'Correctly written dialogue'.
Extension: Encourage children to swap their written dialogues with other children and use them as scripts to perform a role play.

Key aspects of learning
Self-awareness: Children will discuss and reflect on their personal responses to the texts.
Communication: Children will develop their ability to discuss as they work collaboratively in paired, group and whole-class contexts. They will communicate outcomes orally, in writing and through ICT if appropriate.

NARRATIVE

Phase ③ Improving sentences

Learning outcome
Children can vary sentences with different techniques to maintain interest.

Success criteria
- I can identify simple and compound sentences.
- I can identify complex sentences.

Setting the context
This activity should be undertaken after the children have revised using adverbs, adverbial phrases and subordinating connectives and clauses to extend and enhance sentences in modelled and shared writing sessions. Remind the children that the repeated use of the same sort of sentences can make their writing dull and that it is important to vary sentence types to maintain a reader's interest. Children should have had the opportunity to compare simple sentences with compound and complex sentences that say the same thing. Invite children to complete the interactive activity 'Identifying sentence types'.

Assessment opportunity
This activity provides an opportunity to assess children's security about the difference between simple, compound and complex sentences. When children have completed the interactive activity, invite them to explain the difference between the sentences in their own words. Make notes on their responses.

Assessment evidence
At levels 2–3, children will mainly be secure at identifying simple and compound sentences and sometimes complex sentences. At levels 4–5, children will be able to identify subordinating clauses in complex sentences. Your notes on the children's oral responses and the completed interactive activity will provide evidence against Reading AF5.

Next steps
Support: Provide children with a mixture of simple, compound and complex sentences and ask them to underline the verbs and circle the commas that separate clauses.
Extension: Invite children to revise a piece of writing done earlier in the unit and find sentences that could be varied to improve the writing.

Key aspects of learning
Self-awareness: Children will discuss and reflect on their personal responses to the texts.
Communication: Children will develop their ability to discuss as they work collaboratively in paired, group and whole-class contexts. They will communicate outcomes orally, in writing and through ICT if appropriate.

Phase ③ Presenting information

Learning outcome
Children can work effectively as part of a group to research a significant author and make a presentation to the class.

Success criteria
● I can contribute to group research.
● I can deliver an oral presentation to the class.

Setting the context
The children work in groups to research and find out information about a significant author, using a variety of text sources. They should work together to share the information and select what to include in a group presentation. They will then deliver their presentations to the class.

Assessment opportunity
Observe children as they work in their research groups. Encourage them to think about how helpful their notes will be when they make their presentations. Ask questions such as: *Are the points grouped logically, for example, details about the author's background, then first writing and so on?* Later, ask them to self-assess the success of their own presentations. What did they do that worked well? What could they improve? As they assess their own presentations, ask questions to draw out their awareness of presentational skills such as: *Did you look at the audience? Could the audience hear you easily? Did everyone in the group have an equal role in the presentation? How helpful were the notes you made in researching the information?* Invite the children to write their top tips for making oral presentations using photocopiable page 'Top tips for giving a presentation' (versions 1 or 2). Children working at levels 2–3 can use version 1 of 'Top tips for giving a presentation'. Use children's Top tips pages to assess their understanding of how to give an effective presentation.

Assessment evidence
At levels 2–3, children should have noted the most obvious points from their research material and used these to present simple facts about the author. At levels 4–5 children may include opinions on the author's viewpoints in their presentations and support these with some textual references and quotations from their research. Make notes on the children's research and presentations to provide evidence against Reading AF2 and AF6.

Next steps
Support: Compare all the tips the children have written and ask them to select the best six tips from all the pages. Use them to make a poster to help children in future presentations.
Extension: Children research their own favourite author individually and present the information using presentation software.

Key aspects of learning
Evaluation: As they read and compare the work of particular authors, children will express and justify their judgements about books and about the author's style.
Enquiry: Children will decide how to answer questions about an author by using different sources of information, surveys of opinion, and so on.
Social skills: Children will participate in an extended group activity. They will take on a clearly defined role in the group, negotiate with others and reach agreement.
Self-awareness: Children will discuss and reflect on their personal responses to the texts.
Communication: Children will develop their ability to discuss as they work collaboratively in paired, group and whole-class contexts. They will communicate outcomes orally, in writing and through ICT if appropriate.

NARRATIVE

Phase ④ Creating tension

Learning outcome
Children know narrative techniques for creating tension.

Success criteria
I can explain how short sentences are used to create tension.

Setting the context
This activity should be carried out when the children have explored the effect of different sentence types on the atmosphere and tone in stories. They should have explored how using short sentences with repetitive words and phrases can create an atmosphere of tension. Working in groups, provide the children with several different adventure stories that have been read in the class. Suggestions for books could include *Kensuke's Kingdom* by Michael Morpurgo, *Someone's Watching, Someone's Waiting* by Jamila Gavin and *Heaven Eyes* by David Almond. Invite the children to choose one of the stories and find part of the story where the excitement or tension builds up. Ask them to describe the passage to the group and identify the techniques the author has used to create the atmosphere.

Assessment opportunity
Observe children as they contribute to their group's discussion and make notes on their responses. Ask the groups to write a group collection of techniques used by the different authors to create a sense of tension or excitement. Children working at levels 2-3 should work with a supporting adult. Invite each group to share their collection of techniques with the class.

Assessment evidence
Children working at levels 2-3 will identify the author's vocabulary that builds tension, for example, in characters' dialogue. At levels 4-5, children can comment on how sentence structure builds tension; for example, the author uses short sentences, single words and so on. Use observation and notes with each group's collection of techniques to make evidence against Reading AF5.

Next steps
Support: Compare all the techniques the groups have noted and make a poster to help children in future writing.
Extension: Invite children to read passages that have a very calm or soothing atmosphere and identify how the author has achieved this contrasting effect.

Key aspects of learning
Evaluation: As they read and compare the work of particular authors, children will express and justify their judgements about books and about the author's style.
Social skills: Children will participate in an extended group activity. They will take on a clearly defined role in the group, negotiate with others and reach agreement.
Self-awareness: Children will discuss and reflect on their personal responses to the texts.
Communication: Children will develop their ability to discuss as they work collaboratively in paired, group and whole-class contexts. They will communicate outcomes orally, in writing and through ICT if appropriate.

Phase ④ Writing a suspense paragraph

Learning outcome
Children can write their own paragraph applying knowledge from reading.

Success criteria
I can write paragraphs using suspense.

Setting the context
This activity should be carried out when the children have explored the effect of different sentence types on the atmosphere and tone in stories. They should have explored how using short sentences with repeated words and phrases can create an atmosphere of tension. Talk with the children about any real-life situations where they have felt scared, tense and frightened. Encourage them to describe what happened without actually saying how they felt about it. Can they convey the feeling through describing the actions in the situation? Invite the children to write a paragraph describing such a situation. Explain that they can be real or imaginary situations. Ask them to use the techniques they have been exploring to build a sense of suspense and tension for their readers.

Assessment opportunity
Invite the children to carry out a peer assessment of each other's work. They can swap their paragraphs with a partner and read each other's work aloud. Ask them to assess the atmosphere in each other's writing using the photocopiable page 'Tension' (versions 1 or 2). Children working at levels 2–3 can use version 1 of the photocopiable page 'Tension'. They should identify which techniques have been used, and find two examples of effective writing. Finally they can describe one aspect for improvement.

Assessment evidence
At levels 2–3, children's will use short sentences to convey tension in their paragraph, but will probably not vary sentence length to a large degree. At levels 4–5 children will use a range of sentence lengths to help create an atmosphere of tension, and use a variety of structures and features such as connectives to build detail. Use the children's written paragraphs and their partner's evaluations on the photocopiable page 'Tension' to provide evidence against Writing AF5 (see also Reading AF5).

Next steps
Support: Ask children to use their partner's evaluation of one thing that could be improved and revise their paragraph accordingly.
Extension: Invite children to develop their paragraphs into a short story.

Key aspects of learning
Self-awareness: Children will discuss and reflect on their personal responses to the texts.
Communication: Children will develop their ability to discuss as they work collaboratively in paired, group and whole-class contexts. They will communicate outcomes orally, in writing and through ICT if appropriate.

NARRATIVE

Periodic assessment

Reading

Learning outcomes
- Children can express their opinion of a story with reference to other work by the same author.
- Children can talk about the distinctive features of an author's style by referring to characters, themes, settings or use of language.

Success criteria
- I can identify a character's motivation and response using evidence from the text.
- I can describe an author's style, referring to two of their works.
- I can compare two works by the same author.

Setting the context
This assessment should be carried out once children have completed Narrative Unit 1. Ensure children have experienced reading, researching and analysing an author's style. Review the work that has been done during the course of this unit and discuss children's achievements with them. Using two of the stories studied during the unit, ask children to complete the review sheet on the photocopiable page 'Narrative 1 Reading assessment'.

Assessment opportunity
Children should complete the photocopiable page making reference to the two stories studied. Invite children to read their comparisons to others and compare each other's thoughts about the chosen author.

Assessment evidence
At levels 2–3, children will summarise the plots to compare the story structures. At levels 4–5, children can comment on and compare authors' styles of writing. Use the children's written and oral outcomes to provide evidence against Reading AF2, AF5 and AF6. Use this activity as well as examples of children's work throughout this unit to make level judgements for Reading.

Periodic assessment

Writing

Learning outcome

Children can write a complete story with a sequence of events arranged into paragraphs, linked with a range of connectives and varying sentence length.

Success criteria
- I can write a complete story using paragraphs, connectives and different sentence lengths.
- I can revise and edit my own writing.

Setting the context
This assessment should be carried out once children have completed Narrative Unit 1. Collect the work that has been completed during the course of Unit 1 and discuss individual children's achievements with them. Ask them to suggest what they found difficult about the work in the unit and what they found easy to accomplish. Make notes of their responses. Ask children to choose a piece of writing from the beginning of the unit and to swap the work with a partner. Tell them to read their partner's work and to describe what they think is needed to polish it. Invite them to revise their own writing, taking account of their partner's comments. Encourage them to add anything needed to the piece to make it into a finished story.

Assessment opportunity
When children have completed their stories, they swap them with their partners again. Invite the partners to evaluate what they have done to polish and extend the original piece of writing. This activity provides an opportunity to assess children's abilities to evaluate their own or another's writing.

Assessment evidence
Compare your own assessment of the children's writing with the children's oral responses of their own achievements and their partner's evaluations of their completed story to provide evidence against Writing AF3. Use this activity as well as examples of children's work throughout this unit to make level judgements for Writing.

Name   Date

Begin at the beginning (1)

- Read the opening of *Alone on a Wide Wide* Sea by Michael Morpurgo.
- Mark characters' names on the sheet.
- Mark places on the sheet.
- Mark descriptive details.
- Then answer the following questions:

1. Who is the narrator of the story?

_____

_____

2. Is the story told in the first or third person?

_____

_____

3. How does the author introduce a second character?

_____

_____

4. Which word best describes the author's style of writing?

dramatic	light-hearted	conversational	humorous

5. Does the story opening make you want to read on? Why?

_____

_____

6. How is this story opening similar to or different from other stories by Michael Morpurgo?

_____

_____

Red
Amber
Green

I can compare different story openings by the same author, identifying similarities and differences.

Alone on a Wide Wide Sea (b)

Evening was coming on by the time we got to Cooper's Station, but we could still see enough. We could see it was a place on its own, way out in the bush, and we could tell it was a farm. I mean you could smell it straightaway, the moment we clambered down off the bus. There were huge sheds all around, and you could hear cattle moving and shifting around inside. And from further away in the gloom there was the sound of a running creek, and ducks quacking raucously. A gramophone record was playing from the nearby farmhouse, which had a tin roof and a verandah all around it. I thought at first that was where we'd all be living, but we were led past it, carrying our suitcases, down a dirt track and into a compound with a fence all around. In the centre of this was a long wooden shed with steps at one end and a verandah.

"Your new home," the man told us, opening the door. I didn't take much notice of him, not then. I was too busy looking around me. The gramophone needle got stuck as I stood there. I can never think of Cooper's Station without that stuttering snatch of a hymn repeating itself remorselessly in my head, "What a friend we have in Jesus, have in Jesus, have in Jesus, have in Jesus". I wasn't to know it then, but it was the eerie overture that heralded the darkest years of my life.

NARRATIVE

Name _____ Date _____

Top tips for giving a presentation (1)

◢ Use your experience of researching and presenting information to write some tips about giving an oral presentation.

◢ Write two tips about your research.

◢ Write two tips about how to speak.

◢ Write two tips about organising a group presentation

The first two have been done to start you off.

Tips

◢ Make clear brief notes of the information.

◢ Group the information logically.

_____

_____

_____

_____

_____

_____

_____

_____

_____

_____

_____

_____

_____

_____

_____

_____

Red
Amber
Green

I can contribute to group research. ☐

I can deliver an oral presentation to the class. ☐

Name	Date

Tension (1)

◼ Mark the level of suspense, fear or excitement in the paragraph using the scale below.

Very high level ┬

High level ┤

Medium ┤

Low level ┤

Not at all tense └─────────────────

◼ Tick the techniques used in the paragraph.

short sentences

repeated words

repeated phrases

questions

powerful verbs

precise adjectives

Two effective things are:

_____

_____

One improvement:

_____

_____

Red
Amber   I can write paragraphs using suspense. ☐
Green

NARRATIVE
UNIT 2 Traditional stories, myths and legends

Literacy objectives

Speak and listen for a wide range of purposes in different contexts
Strand 1 Speaking
- Tell a story using notes designed to cue techniques, such as repetition, recap and humour.

Strand 4 Drama
- Reflect on how working in role helps to explore complex issues.
- Perform a scripted scene making use of dramatic conventions.

Read and write for a range of purposes on paper and on screen
Strand 6 Word structure and spelling
- Know and use less common prefixes and suffixes such as *im-, ir-, -cian.*

Strand 7 Understanding and interpreting texts
- Make notes on and use evidence from across a text to explain events or ideas.
- Compare different types of narrative and information texts and identify how they are structured.
- Explore how writers use language for comic and dramatic effects.

Strand 8 Engaging with and responding to texts
- Compare the usefulness of techniques such as visualisation, prediction and empathy in exploring the meaning of texts.

Strand 9 Creating and shaping texts
- Reflect independently and critically on their own writing and edit and improve it.
- Experiment with different narrative form and styles to write own stories.

Strand 10 Text structure and organisation
- Experiment with the order of sections and paragraphs to achieve different effects.

Strand 11 Sentence structure and punctuation
- Punctuate sentences accurately, including using speech marks and apostrophes.
- Adapt sentence structure to different text-types, purposes and readers.

Key aspects of learning

Enquiry
- Children will investigate a range of narrative texts by asking relevant questions and research and then plan and present these narratives orally and in writing.

Creative thinking
- Children will generate and extend imaginative ideas to create a narrative. They will suggest hypotheses, responding imaginatively through drama and talk, and respond to problems in order to create a written outcome.

Communication
- Children will develop their skills to reflect critically on what they have seen and read. They will develop their ability to present a narrative for different audiences, orally and in writing, and reflect critically on their own and others' work.

Assessment focuses

Reading
AF2 (*understand, describe, select or retrieve information, events or ideas from texts and use quotation and reference to text*).
AF4 (*identify and comment on the structure and organisation of texts, including grammatical and presentational features at text level*).
AF5 (*explain and comment on writers' use of language, including grammatical and literary features at word and sentence level*).
AF6 (*identify and comment on writers' purposes and viewpoints, and the overall effect of the text on the reader*).
AF7 (*relate texts to their social, cultural and historical contexts and literary traditions*).

Writing
AF2 (*produce texts which are appropriate to task, reader and purpose*).
AF3 (*organise and present whole texts effectively, sequencing and structuring information, ideas and events*).
AF5 (*vary sentences for clarity, purpose and effect*).

Speaking and listening
Speaking (speak with clarity; adapt intonation and pace and use oral techniques).
Drama (collaborate to give a group performance; identify qualities of others' performance).

Resources

Phase 1 activities
Interactive activity, 'Traditional stories, myths and legends'
Photocopiable page, 'Compare and contrast' (versions 1 and 2)
Phase 2 activities
Photocopiable page, 'Speech'
Interactive activity, 'Speech'
Photocopiable page, 'Iroquois creation myth'
Photocopiable page, 'The structure and features of a creation myth' (versions 1 and 2)
Photocopiable page, 'Pandora's Box '
Interactive activity, 'Pandora's Box'
Phase 3 activities
Photocopiable page, 'Group plan' (versions 1 and 2)
Phase 4 activities
Photocopiable page, 'A new hero' (versions 1 and 2)
Photocopiable page, 'Story plan' (versions 1 and 2)
Periodic assessment
Interactive activity, 'Narrative 2 Reading assessment'
Recommended texts
The Story of Mulan: The Daughter and Warrior by Gang Yi and Xiao Guo (ISBN 978-0974-48400-6)
Mulan: a Pantomime by Richard Hills (ISBN 978-1902-83711-6)
'Persephone' from *Play Time: A Selection of Plays* by Julia Donaldson (ISBN 978-0330-44595-5)
Robin Hood audiobook read by John Nettles (ISBN 978-0140-86791-6)
Robin Hood Junior Classics audiobook read by John McAndrew (ISBN 978-9626-34692-1)
King Arthur and the Knights of the Round Table audiobook read by Sean Bean (ISBN 978-9626-34138-4).

Unit 2 ⬜ Traditional stories, myths and legends

Learning outcomes	Assessment opportunity and evidence	Assessment focuses (AFs)		Success criteria
		Level 2	Level 3	
Phase ① activities pages 34-35				
Key features Children demonstrate that they can classify features of different fiction genres.	● Paired and group activity where children brainstorm the features of myths, legends and fairy tales and complete an interactive activity. ● Group oral feedback and completed interactive activities.	**Reading AF7** ● General features of a few text types identified. ● Some awareness that books are set in different times and places.	**Reading AF7** ● Some simple connections between texts identified. ● Recognition of some features of the context of texts.	I can identify the different features of myths, traditional stories and legends.
Comparing stories Children can describe the similarities and differences between different versions of the same story and support their opinions by referring to evidence in the text.	● Independent activity where children compare and contrast three versions of the same story. ● Children's oral responses and written responses on the photocopiable page.	**Reading AF7** ● General features of a few text types identified. ● Some awareness that books are set in different times and places.	**Reading AF7** ● Some simple connections between texts identified. ● Recognition of some features of the context of texts.	I can identify the similarities and differences between different versions of the same story.
Phase ② activities pages 36-38				
Speech Children can understand the difference between direct and reported speech.	● Independent activity where children identify examples of direct and reported speech and comment on its different uses. ● Children's completed interactive activities and oral responses.	**Reading AF5** ● Some effective language choices noted. ● Some familiar patterns of language identified.	**Reading AF5** ● A few basic features of writer's use of language identified, but with little or no comment.	● I can recognise direct and reported speech. ● I can change reported speech to direct speech and vice versa.
The structure of a myth Children can identify different features and the structure of a myth.	● Independent activity where children listen to and read a creation myth and demonstrate their understanding of its structure and features in comparison with other myths. ● Children's oral responses and written responses on the photocopiable page.	**Reading AF2** ● Some specific, straightforward information recalled. ● Generally clear idea of where to look for information.	**Reading AF2** ● Simple, most obvious points identified though there may also be some misunderstanding. ● Some comments include quotations from or references to text, but not always relevant.	I can identify the structure and features of a creation myth.
Paragraph order Children can see how paragraph order can affect the reader and narrative viewpoint.	● Independent activity where children listen to a reading of 'Pandora's Box' and re-order paragraphs to justify her actions. ● Notes against the class list of children's evaluations and the completed interactive activity.	**Reading AF4** ● Some awareness of use of features of organisation. **Reading AF6** ● Some awareness that writers have viewpoints and purposes. ● Simple statements about likes and dislikes in reading, sometimes with reasons.	**Reading AF4** ● A few basic features of organisation at text level identified, with little or no linked comment. **Reading AF6** ● Comments identify main purpose. ● Express personal response but with little awareness of writer's viewpoint or effect on reader.	I can experiment with the order of paragraphs in writing.

Unit 2 ▭ Traditional stories, myths and legends

Learning outcomes	Assessment opportunity and evidence	Assessment focuses (AFs)		Success criteria
		Level 2	Level 3	
Phase ③ activities pages 39-40				
Storytelling techniques Children demonstrate use of techniques to engage and interest an audience when retelling a legend orally.	● Independent activity where children listen to two readings of the same extract and note good storytelling techniques. ● Children's oral responses and notes made against the class list.	**Reading AF6** ● Some awareness that writers have viewpoints and purposes. ● Simple statements about likes and dislikes in reading, sometimes with reasons.	**Reading AF6** ● Comments identify main purpose. ● Express personal response but with little awareness of writer's viewpoint or effect on reader.	● I can identify the features of oral and written versions. ● I can retell a known myth using oral techniques.
Plan an oral storytelling ● Children can plan their own version of a legend. ● Children can retell a legend orally, using their own notes to support them. ● Children demonstrate use of techniques to engage and interest an audience when retelling a legend orally.	● Supported group activity where children plan an oral retelling of a legend, perform it for the class and evaluate each other's work. ● Oral peer evaluations and notes made on the photocopiable page.	**Writing AF2** ● Some basic purpose established. ● Some appropriate features of the given form used. ● Some attempts to adopt appropriate style.	**Writing AF2** ● Purpose established at a general level. ● Main features of selected form sometimes signalled to the reader. ● Some attempts at appropriate style, with attention to reader.	● I can plan a retelling of a known legend using oral techniques. ● I can use techniques to engage and interest the audience.
Phase ④ activities pages 41-42				
Heroes Children can identify the characteristics of their mythical hero.	● Paired activity where children create a new hero for a myth or a legend, then evaluate each other's ideas. ● Children's written outcomes on the photocopiable page and paired evaluations.	**Writing AF2** ● Some basic purpose established. ● Some appropriate features of the given form used. ● Some attempts to adopt appropriate style.	**Writing AF2** ● Purpose established at a general level. ● Main features of selected form sometimes signalled to the reader. ● Some attempts at appropriate style, with attention to reader.	I can identify the characteristics of heroes.
Planning a myth or legend ● Children can write a new version of a legend, identifying their audience and adapting their writing to suit this audience. ● Children can reflect critically on their own writing and edit and improve it.	● Paired activity where children plan a new version of a myth or legend using a writing frame and then evaluate their work. ● Children's oral evaluations and written outcomes on the photocopiable page.	**Writing AF3** ● Some basic sequencing of ideas or material. ● Openings and/or closings sometimes signalled.	**Writing AF3** ● Some attempt to organise ideas with related points placed next to each other. ● Openings and closings usually signalled. ● Some attempt to sequence ideas or material logically.	● I can plan my own version of a myth or legend. ● I can reflect critically on my own writing.

Unit 2 Traditional stories, myths and legends

Learning outcomes	Assessment opportunity and evidence	Assessment focuses (AFs)		Success criteria
		Level 4	Level 5	
Phase ① activities pages 34-35				
Key features Children demonstrate that they can classify features of different fiction genres.	• Independent and group activity where children brainstorm the features of myths, legends and fairy tales and complete an interactive activity. • Group oral feedback and completed interactive activities.	**Reading AF7** • Features common to different texts or versions of the same text identified, with simple comment. • Simple comment on the effect that the reader's or writer's context has on the meaning of texts.	**Reading AF7** • Comments identify similarities and differences between texts, or versions, with some explanation. • Some explanation of how the contexts in which texts are written and read contribute to meaning.	I can identify the different features of myths, traditional stories and legends.
Comparing stories Children can describe the similarities and differences between different versions of the same story and support their opinions by referring to evidence in the text.	• Independent activity where children compare and contrast three versions of the same story. • Children's oral responses and written responses on the photocopiable page.	**Reading AF7** • Features common to different texts or versions of the same text identified, with simple comment. • Simple comment on the effect that the reader's or writer's context has on the meaning of texts.	**Reading AF7** • Comments identify similarities and differences between texts, or versions, with some explanation. • Some explanation of how the contexts in which texts are written and read contribute to meaning.	I can identify the similarities and differences between different versions of the same story.
Phase ② activities pages 36-38				
Speech Children can understand the difference between direct and reported speech.	• Independent activity where children identify examples of direct and reported speech and comment on its different uses. • Children's oral responses and written responses on the photocopiable page.	**Writing AF5** • Some variety in length, structure or subject of sentences. • Use of some subordinating connectives throughout the text. • Some variation, generally accurate, in tense and verb forms.	**Writing AF5** • A variety of sentence lengths, structures and subjects provides clarity and emphasis. • Wider range of connectives used to clarify relationship between ideas. • Some features of sentence structure used to build up detail or convey shades of meaning.	• I can recognise direct and reported speech. • I can change reported speech to direct speech and vice versa.
The structure of a myth Children can identify different features and the structure of a myth.	• Independent activity where children listen to and read a creation myth and demonstrate their understanding of its structure and features in comparison with other myths. • Children's oral and written responses.	**Reading AF2** • Some relevant points identified. • Comments supported by some generally relevant textual reference or quotation.	**Reading AF2** • Most relevant points clearly identified, including those selected from different places in the text. • Comments generally supported by relevant textual reference or quotation, even when points made are not always accurate.	I can identify the structure and features of a creation myth.
Paragraph order Children can see how paragraph order can affect the reader and narrative viewpoint.	• Independent activity where children listen to a reading of 'Pandora's Box' and re-order paragraphs to justify her actions. • Notes against the class list of children's evaluations and the completed interactive activity.	**Reading AF4** • Some structural choices identified with simple comment. • Some basic features of organisation at text level identified. **Reading AF6** • Main purpose identified. • Simple comments show some awareness of writer's viewpoint. • Simple comment on overall effect on reader.	**Reading AF4** • Comments on structural choices show some general awareness of writer's craft. • Various features relating to organisation at text level, including form, are clearly identified, with some explanation. **Reading AF6** • Main purpose clearly identified, often through general overview. • Viewpoint in texts clearly identified, with some, often limited, explanation. • General awareness of effect on the reader, with some, often limited, explanation.	I can experiment with the order of paragraphs in writing.

Unit 2 Traditional stories, myths and legends

Phase 3 activities pages 39–40

Storytelling techniques Children demonstrate use of techniques to engage and interest an audience when retelling a legend orally.	• Independent activity where children listen to two readings of the same extract and note good storytelling techniques. • Children's oral responses and notes made against the class list.	**Reading AF6** • Main purpose identified. • Simple comments show some awareness of writer's viewpoint. • Simple comment on overall effect on reader.	**Reading AF6** • Main purpose clearly identified, often through general overview. • Viewpoint in texts clearly identified, with some, often limited, explanation. • General awareness of effect on the reader, with some, often limited, explanation.	• I can identify the features of oral and written versions. • I can retell a known myth using oral techniques.
Plan an oral storytelling • Children can plan their own version of a legend. • Children can retell a legend orally, using their own notes to support them. • Children demonstrate use of techniques to engage and interest an audience when retelling a legend orally.	• Group activity where children plan an oral retelling of a legend, perform it for the class and evaluate each other's work. • Notes against the class list of children's evaluations and written responses on the photocopiable page.	**Writing AF2** • Main purpose of writing is clear but not always consistently maintained. • Main features of selected form are clear and appropriate to purpose. • Style generally appropriate to task, though awareness of reader not always sustained.	**Writing AF2** • Main purpose of writing is clear and consistently maintained. • Features of selected form clearly established with some adaptation to purpose. • Appropriate style clearly established to maintain reader's interest throughout.	• I can plan a retelling of a known legend using oral techniques. • I can use techniques to engage and interest the audience.

Phase 4 activities pages 41–42

Heroes Children can identify the characteristics of their mythical hero.	• Paired activity where children create a new hero for a myth or a legend, then evaluate each other's ideas. • Children's written outcomes on the photocopiable page and paired evaluations.	**Writing AF2** • Main purpose of writing is clear but not always consistently maintained. • Main features of selected form are clear and appropriate to purpose. • Style generally appropriate to task, though awareness of reader not always sustained.	**Writing AF2** • Main purpose of writing is clear and consistently maintained. • Features of selected form clearly established with some adaptation to purpose. • Appropriate style clearly established to maintain reader's interest throughout.	I can identify the characteristics of heroes.
Planning a myth or legend • Children can write a new version of a legend, identifying their audience and adapting their writing to suit this audience. • Children can reflect critically on their own writing and edit and improve it.	• Paired activity where children plan a new version of a myth or legend using a writing frame and then evaluate their work. • Independent activity where children plan a new version of a myth or legend using a writing frame and then evaluate their work. • Children's oral evaluations and written outcomes on the photocopiable page.	**Writing AF3** • Ideas organised by clustering related points or by time sequence. • Ideas are organised simply with a fitting opening and closing, sometimes linked. • Ideas or material generally in logical sequence but overall direction of writing not always clearly signalled.	**Writing AF3** • Material is structured clearly, with sentences organised into appropriate paragraphs. • Development of material is effectively managed across text. • Overall direction of the text supported by clear links between paragraphs.	• I can plan my own version of a myth or legend. • I can reflect critically on my own writing.

NARRATIVE

Phase ① Key features

Learning outcome
Children demonstrate that they can classify features of different fiction genres.

Success criteria
I can identify the different features of myths, traditional stories and legends.

Setting the context
This activity should be carried out once children have read and explored the key features of myths, legends and other traditional stories in shared, guided and independent reading. They should have compared and contrasted typical characters, settings and plot structures, use of language and dialogue and purposes. Arrange the children into small groups of similar ability. Provide them with three sheets of paper, one headed 'Myths', one headed 'Legends' and one headed 'Fairy tales'. Ask them to hold a short brainstorming session and write all the things they know about the three genres on the appropriate sheet. Now explain that they are going to do the interactive activity 'Traditional stories, myths and legends' which features typical elements of myths, legends and fairy tales. Children select which genre each feature belongs to.

Assessment opportunity
Ask each group to feedback their results from the brainstorming session. For the interactive activity, children working at levels 4-5 will work independently to read and answer the questions. Children working at levels 2-3 should work in pairs. Observe as they discuss and make notes of their contributions.

Assessment evidence
At levels 2-3, children will be able to add detail to the features of myths and fairy tales, such as a hero and monster-villains in myths and legends. Children working at levels 4-5 will comment also on the author's use of language, such as story-teller language based on the oral origins of traditional stories. Use notes made against the class list of group feedback/paired responses and the completed interactive to provide evidence for Reading AF7 (see also Reading AF4).

Next steps
Support: Provide a list of key features of myths, legends and fairy tales. Give children a different myth, legend or fairy tale to read at home each day and ask them to make notes of the features in the story that help them classify the genre. Ask them to describe the reasons for their answer orally.
Extension: Provide children with a myth, legend or fable. Invite them to identify the genre and write a paragraph describing the features.

Key aspects of learning
Enquiry: Children will investigate a range of narrative texts by asking relevant questions and research and then plan and present these narratives orally and in writing.
Communication: Children will develop their skills to reflect critically on what they have seen and read. They will develop their ability to present a narrative for different audiences, orally and in writing, and reflect critically on their own and others' work.

Phase ① Comparing stories

Learning outcome
Children can describe the similarities and differences between different versions of the same story and support their opinions by referring to evidence in the text.

Success criteria
I can identify the similarities and differences between different versions of the same story.

Setting the context
This activity should be undertaken once children have explored the features of myths, legends and other traditional stories, such as fairy tales. They should have had the opportunity to compare and contrast the treatment of similar themes in the same and in different genres and the ways in which language has been used. Provide the children with copies of the same story told in different versions, for example, a narrative story, a play and a film version. Suitable texts might be: *The Story of Mulan: The Daughter and Warrior*, written by Gang Yi and Xiao Guo; *Mulan*, a Pantomime written by Richard Hills; any versions of 'Persephone and the Pomegranate Seed', such as 'Persephone' from *Play Time* a selection of plays by Julia Donaldson. Over several days, read the texts and watch the film. Provide the children with the photocopiable page 'Compare and contrast (versions 1 and 2)' and ask them to make notes to compare and contrast the stories. Children working at levels 2-3 can use version 1 of the photocopiable page.

Assessment opportunity
Ask children to use their page of notes to give feedback about their findings. Draw out their responses with questioning, for example: *How much from the narrative story is included in the play and film? How does this affect your enjoyment of the story? Which version appealed most to you and why?* Make notes of their oral responses.

Assessment evidence
At levels 2-3, children will select general features from a list. At levels 4-5, children will identify common features and will comment critically about the audience and purpose of different versions. Use children's oral responses and completed photocopiable pages to provide evidence against Reading AF7 (see also Reading AF6).

Next steps
Support: For children who struggled to make comparisons, run the activity again using only two different versions of a story.
Extension: Invite children to write a review of the book, play or film version that they preferred most.

Key aspects of learning
Communication: Children will develop their skills to reflect critically on what they have seen and read. They will develop their ability to present a narrative for different audiences, orally and in writing, and reflect critically on their own and others' work.

NARRATIVE

Phase ② Speech

Learning outcome
Children can understand the difference between direct and reported speech.

Success criteria
● I can recognise direct and reported speech.
● I can change reported speech to direct speech and vice versa.

Setting the context
This activity should be carried out after the children have explored the use of dialogue in stories in shared and guided reading and writing. They should have revised the rules for writing, punctuating and laying out dialogue. They should have explored how direct speech is used in myths, legends and traditional stories and when an author chooses to use reported speech using the voice of the narrator rather than the character. Ask the children working at levels 2-3 to do the interactive activity 'Speech'. Provide children working at levels 4-5 with the photocopiable page 'Speech' and ask them to complete it, which will improve identifying each type of speech and changing the speech type from direct speech to reported speech and vice versa.

Assessment opportunity
This activity provides the opportunity to assess whether children are secure in their understanding of direct and reported speech. When children have completed the activities, ask them to say when and why they would use reported speech and direct speech in their own writing. Responses might include ideas such as: *varying the use of sentence structures to maintain readers' interest in fiction; direct speech can convey how the words are spoken through powerful speech verbs; reported speech is better suited to writing recounts and journalistic text.*

Assessment evidence
Use the completed interactive activities to provide evidence against Reading AF5, for children at levels 2-3. At levels 4-5, the children's completed photocopiable pages can be used to provide evidence against Writing AF5 (see also Writing AF6).

Next steps
Support: Children who confuse direct and reported speech should be given the opportunity to revise the layout and conventions of speech punctuation.
Extension: Encourage children to change the direct speech in a passage from a myth they have been reading and comment on the effect on the text.

Key aspects of learning
Communication: Children will develop their skills to reflect critically on what they have seen and read. They will develop their ability to present a narrative for different audiences, orally and in writing, and reflect critically on their own and others' work.

Phase ② The structure of a myth

Learning outcome
Children can identify different features and the structure of a myth.

Success criteria
I can identify the structure and features of a creation myth.

Setting the context
This activity should be undertaken after the children have had the opportunity to compare the structure of different types of myths and legends, including creation myths from different cultures, in shared and guided reading. Read the photocopiable page 'Iroquois creation myth'. Explain that many Native American cultures, like the Iroquois tribe, believed in many different 'spirits' who lived on an island in the sky and that they believe dreams are very important. Provide the children with copies of the myth and of photocopiable page 'The structure and features of a creation myth (version 1 or 2)' and ask them to answer the six questions about the structure and features of the myth. Children working at levels 2-3 should use version 1 of the photocopiable page.

Assessment opportunity
This activity provides an opportunity to assess children's security about the features and structure of creation myths. When children have completed the photocopiable page, ask them to describe the common key elements of a creation myth that features in the Iroquois myth. Ask questions of children working at lower levels to draw out their responses, for example: *Is this belief common to everyone or just the people who invented the myth? Are there any other myths you have read where someone 'falls' from one place to another and takes something special with him or her? In which other myths does something evil come into the world? Is this evil ever driven out completely?*

Assessment evidence
At levels 2-3, children answer with direct evidence from the text, for example: 'Sky woman fell because she slipped through the hole'. At levels 4-5, children will use inferences, for example: 'Sky woman fell because she was curious'. Make notes of children's oral responses and use the completed photocopiable pages to provide evidence against Reading AF2 (see also Reading AF3 and AF4).

Next steps
Support: Invite children to read other examples of creation myths, for example, from Aboriginal, Chinese and African cultures and compare the common features, such as what is created, what causes evil, how evil is overcome.
Extension: Invite children to draw up a list of 'essential features' for writing a creation myth. Compile their answers into a poster to display in the classroom.

Key aspects of learning
Communication: Children will develop their skills to reflect critically on what they have seen and read. They will develop their ability to present a narrative for different audiences, orally and in writing, and reflect critically on their own and others' work.

NARRATIVE

Phase ② Paragraph order

Learning outcome
Children can see how paragraph order can affect the reader and narrative viewpoint.

Success criteria
I can experiment with the order of paragraphs in writing.

Setting the context
This activity should be undertaken after the children have had the opportunity to experiment with the order of paragraphs in shared, guided and independent writing. They should be aware that the order of paragraphs can strengthen or weaken their desired effect on the reader. Ensure the children are familiar with the myth of Pandora's box before they begin the activity, by reading the story on the photocopiable page 'Pandora's Box'. Children working at levels 4–5 can read the text independently. Explain that Pandora's justification for what she did is explained in the interactive activity 'Pandora's Box'. Children are to re-order the paragraphs to put Pandora's point of view as forcefully as possible. Remind the children that putting positive ideas before negative ideas can influence the reader's thoughts about an issue.

Assessment opportunity
When children have re-ordered the paragraphs, ask them to read the passage aloud and compare their answers. Ask them which order makes them feel the most sympathy with Pandora and how the order affects their opinions. Make notes of children's responses.

Assessment evidence
At levels 2–3, children will tend to choose the order of paragraphs based on Pandora's statements beginning with the first person, and sometimes randomly. At levels 4–5, pupils will be more aware of the persuasive purpose and so use positive statements to lead the order. Use your notes and the completed interactive activity to provide evidence against Reading AF4 and AF6.

Next steps
Support: Provide children with 'Pandora's Box' or another myth cut into paragraphs and ask them to arrange the paragraphs.
Extension: Invite children to write a justification for another character associated with temptation, for example, Adam and Eve in the Garden of Eden. They should use what they have learnt about paragraph order when undertaking this.

Key aspects of learning
Communication: Children will develop their skills to reflect critically on what they have seen and read. They will develop their ability to present a narrative for different audiences, orally and in writing, and reflect critically on their own and others' work.

■SCHOLASTIC

Phase ③ Storytelling techniques

Learning outcome
Children demonstrate use of techniques to engage and interest an audience when retelling a legend orally.

Success criteria
● I can identify the features of oral and written versions.
● I can retell a known myth using oral techniques.

Setting the context
This activity should be carried out when the children have read and explored the features of myths and legends in shared, guided and independent reading and identified the features of good stories such as a clear theme, a well-developed plot, vivid use of language and characterisation. Read a chapter of a well-known legend to the class, such as 'Robin Hood' or 'King Arthur', without much expression or animation in your voice and then ask them to listen to the same story read by a storyteller on a CD or audio-tape. Suitable examples are *Robin Hood* audio book, read by John Nettles, *Robin Hood* Junior Classics audio book, read by John McAndrew or *King Arthur and the Knights of the Round Table,* read by Sean Bean. Ask the children as they listen to make notes of the techniques used by the storyteller compared with your own reading.

Assessment opportunity
Children working at levels 2–3, will identify how changes in tone of voice, expression or volume are used to emphasise the author's viewpoint and intended effect on the audience. Children working at levels 4–5 will note changes in pace and use of pauses. Invite the children to give oral feedback of their ideas about how the storyteller engaged their interest. Discuss their ideas and make notes of their responses.

Assessment evidence
At levels 2–3, children will be able to recognise and identify general features of the texts. At levels 4–5 children will identify and comment on similar features in versions of the same texts and will make simple comments on the effect of the oral story-telling on them as listeners/readers. Use children's oral responses and discussion and notes made against the class list to make evidence against Reading AF6.

Next steps
Support: Draw up a list of storytelling techniques and display them. Provide other stories as audiobooks and ask the children to listen for the techniques on the list.
Extension: Invite children to read their own stories to a partner using some of the techniques identified.

Key aspects of learning
Communication: Children will develop their skills to reflect critically on what they have seen and read. They will develop their ability to present a narrative for different audiences, orally and in writing, and reflect critically on their own and others' work.

NARRATIVE

Phase ③ Plan an oral storytelling

Learning outcomes
- Children can plan their own version of a legend.
- Children can retell a legend orally using their own notes to support them.
- Children demonstrate use of techniques to engage and interest an audience when retelling a legend orally.

Success criteria
- I can plan a retelling of a known legend using oral techniques.
- I can use techniques to engage and interest the audience.

Setting the context
This activity should be carried out when the children have listened to oral versions of legends and explored the techniques used to engage an audience in oral storytelling, such as varying tone of voice and pace, using pauses to create suspense, repeating words and phrases, often in groups of three, asking direct questions, using 'asides'. Arrange the children into small groups of similar ability with children working at levels 2–3 supported by an adult. Ask them to plan a group oral version of one of the legends they have been studying during the unit. Provide them with the photocopiable page 'Group plan' (versions 1 or 2) and ask them to make notes as prompts for the opening, middle and ending of the legend. Children working at levels 2–3 can use version 1 of the photocopiable page.

Assessment opportunity
Allow a short period of time for the groups to rehearse their legends and invite the groups to perform their oral retellings for the class using their notes as prompts. When each group finishes, ask the children who are listening to identify which techniques have been used, and find two examples that worked well. Finally they can describe one aspect for improvement.

Assessment evidence
Children working at levels 2–3 might need to read from their notes. They will generally use the characters' names correctly and choose some simple events to retell the story. But they may struggle to link the events effectively and to link smoothly between members of the group and their relevant parts. They should use some simple story-teller language. Children at levels 4–5 use their notes as prompts and expand them to tell the story. They will have chosen and sequenced the events to retell the legend well and should include a variety of thought out story-teller language. Use the children's evaluations and the written notes on the photocopiable page to provide evidence against Writing AF2 and (see also Writing AF5).

Next steps
Support: Ask children to choose one storytelling technique only and use it to retell a familiar traditional tale to build confidence in storytelling.
Extension: Invite individual children to tell a story they are familiar with.

Key aspects of learning
Enquiry: Children will investigate a range of narrative texts by asking relevant questions and research and then plan and present these narratives orally and in writing.
Communication: Children will develop their skills to reflect critically on what they have seen and read. They will develop their ability to present a narrative for different audiences, orally and in writing, and reflect critically on their own and others' work.

Phase ④ Heroes

Learning outcome
Children can identify the characteristics of their mythical hero.

Success criteria
I can identify the characteristics of heroes.

Setting the context
This activity should be carried out when the children have read and explored different myths and legends that feature hero figures such as Jason, Hercules, Achilles, Pandora, Robin Hood, Marion and King Arthur. They should have studied the typical characteristics of each hero - their appearance, strengths and weaknesses and special characteristics. Provide the children with copies of the photocopiable page 'A new hero (versions 1 or 2)'. Ask them to create a new hero for a new myth or legend. Children working at levels 2-3 should draw and label their hero figure using version 1 of the photocopiable page.

Assessment opportunity
When they have completed the character description, invite the children to work with a partner and, using their photocopiable sheets, give their partner an oral description of their new hero. Ask the partners then to feed back two things about the character that will make them a good hero and one thing that could be developed and improved.

Assessment evidence
At levels 2-3, children will be able to provide descriptions of the hero's physical appearance. At levels 4-5, children will also describe aspects of the hero's personal qualities. Make notes of the pairs' comments. Use these and the completed photocopiable pages to provide evidence against Writing AF2.

Next steps
Support: Ask children to develop their hero in the light of their partner's evaluations.
Extension: Invite children to repeat the activity to describe a companion or partner for their hero.

Key aspects of learning
Enquiry: Children will investigate a range of narrative texts by asking relevant questions and research and then plan and present these narratives orally and in writing.
Creative thinking: Children will generate and extend imaginative ideas to create a narrative. They will suggest hypotheses, responding imaginatively through drama and talk, and respond to problems in order to create a written outcome.
Communication: Children will develop their skills to reflect critically on what they have seen and read. They will develop their ability to present a narrative for different audiences, orally and in writing, and reflect critically on their own and others' work.

NARRATIVE

Phase ④ Planning a myth or legend

Learning outcomes
- Children can write a new version of a legend, identifying their audience and adapting their writing to suit this audience.
- Children can reflect critically on their own writing and edit and improve it.

Success criteria
- I can plan my own version of a myth or legend.
- I can reflect critically on my own writing.

Setting the context
This activity should be carried out when the children have had the opportunity to plan a legend or a myth in modelled, shared and guided writing. Remind them that all stories should have a clear opening, a problem, a build up and the problem resolved. There should also be a clear ending. Explain that they are going to write brief notes to plan how to write their own version of a known legend or myth using the photocopiable page 'Story plan (version 1 or 2)'. Children working at levels 2–3 should use version 1 of the photocopiable page and collaborate with a partner to write their notes.

Assessment opportunity
When they have completed the photocopiable page, invite the children to give an oral description of their myth or legend. Ask them to say what they found easy to do and what they found challenging. Encourage them to reflect critically by asking: *Would you change anything about your legend? If so, what? What might you add to your notes to improve your legend?* Make notes of their oral responses.

Assessment evidence
At levels 2–3, children will describe a simple beginning, middle and ending. At levels 4–5, children will provide greater detail about characters and plot in their story plans which will be organised in a generally logical sequence. Use children's written outcomes, oral self-evaluations and notes to provide evidence for Writing AF3.

Next steps
Support: For children who struggled, invite them to work in a group and discuss a group story. Reduce the number of challenges for their hero and divide the stages of the story so that each child concentrates on only one part.
Extension: Allow time for children to improve their notes and then invite them to turn their notes into a polished story.

Key aspects of learning
Enquiry: Children will investigate a range of narrative texts by asking relevant questions and research and then plan and present these narratives orally and in writing.
Creative thinking: Children will generate and extend imaginative ideas to create a narrative. They will suggest hypotheses, responding imaginatively through drama and talk, and respond to problems in order to create a written outcome.
Communication: Children will develop their skills to reflect critically on what they have seen and read. They will develop their ability to present a narrative for different audiences, orally and in writing, and reflect critically on their own and others' work.

Periodic assessment

Reading

Learning outcome Children can identify the different features of traditional stories, myths and legends.	**Success criteria** I can classify the features of traditional stories, myths and legends. **Setting the context** Ensure children have experience analysing the different genres. Review the work that has been done during the course of this unit and discuss children's achievements with them. Ask them what they found easy to accomplish and what was difficult. Make notes of their responses. Invite the children to show their understanding of the different genres by completing the interactive activity 'Narrative 2 Reading assessment'. **Assessment opportunity** This assessment provides the opportunity for children to evaluate their own understanding of the structure and features of traditional stories, myths and legends. The interactive activity will enable children to assess their abilities to differentiate between three genres. **Assessment evidence** Children working at levels 2–3 might demonstrate greater difficulty in discriminating between the features of myths and legends than those working at levels 4–5. Use children's oral self-assessments and the completed interactive activity to provide evidence against Reading AF4 and AF7.

Writing

Learning outcomes ● Children can write a new version of a myth or legend, identifying their audience and adapting their writing to suit this audience. ● Children can reflect critically on their own writing and edit and improve it.	**Success criteria** ● I can write myths and legends. ● I can reflect critically on my own writing. **Setting the context** Collect the work that has been completed during the course of the unit and discuss individual children's achievements with them. Ask them to suggest what they found difficult about the writing in the unit and what they found easy to accomplish. Make notes of their responses. Ask children to choose a piece of writing done at the beginning of the unit and to swap it with a partner. Tell them to read their partner's work and describe what they think is needed to polish it. Invite them to revise their own writing, taking account of what they have learned during the whole unit and their partner's comments. **Assessment opportunity** When children have completed their myths or legends, they swap them with their partners again. Invite the partners to evaluate what they have done to polish and extend the original piece of writing. This activity provides an opportunity to assess children's abilities to evaluate their own or another's writing. Make notes of how children's peer evaluations differ from your own evaluations and plan appropriate action for the next unit. **Assessment evidence** Children's oral responses and their partner's evaluations of their completed myth or legend will provide evidence against Writing AF1. Use this activity and children's work throughout the unit to make level judgements for Writing.

Iroquois creation myth

nce, before the world we know existed, the Spirits lived on an island, floating in the sky, where the ruler of the Sky Island, Great Spirit, had a wife who was expecting his baby. One night she had a dream that the Celestial Tree, from which grew all the fruit and flowers for the island, was uprooted. She told her husband of the dream. Realising that the dream was a powerful message, he at once uprooted the tree, leaving a great hole in the middle of the island. But when his curious wife peered into the hole, she slipped and tumbled through, down towards the waters below. As she slipped, she grabbed a handful of seeds from the branches of the Celestial Tree.

Animals already existed in the water. So, far below the floating island, two birds saw the Sky Woman fall. They caught her on their backs, just before she plunged into the water, and brought her to the other animals. Trying to help the woman, they dived into the water to get mud from the bottom of the seas. One after another the animals tried and failed. Finally, Little Toad tried and returned with a single mouthful of mud. The other animals took it and spread it on the back of Big Turtle. The mud began to grow and grow and grow until it became the whole world.

Then the woman stepped onto the land. She sprinkled the seeds onto the ground and from them grew all the plants of the earth.

Then Sky Woman gave birth to a daughter, who married the West Wind and in time, gave birth to twin sons. She named one Sapling. He grew up to be kind and caring. She named the other Flint and his heart was as cold as his name. They grew quickly and began filling the earth with their creations.

Sapling created all that is good. He taught the birds to sing and fish to leap. He made rivers, soft rain and rainbows.

However, Flint was jealous and tried to destroy Sapling's work and made all that is bad. He made the rapids in the rivers. He created poisonous plants. He created monsters which his brother drove beneath the Earth.

At last, Sapling decided Flint should be driven out. He challenged him to a fight and Flint was beaten. As he was a god, Flint could not die, so he was banished to live under the land. He still shows his anger in the eruptions of volcanoes.

Illustration © 2009, Simon Smith/Beehive Illustration.

Name _____   Date _____

The structure and features of a creation myth (1)

1. Do you think this story tells how the world was really created?

Yes ☐   ☐ No

2. Why did Sky Woman fall? _____

_____

_____

3. How does Sky Woman create trees and plants? _____

_____

_____

4. How does evil come into the new world? _____

_____

_____

5. Who defeats the evil? _____

_____

_____

6. What happens to Flint? _____

_____

_____

_____

Red ⬤
Amber ⬤   I can identify the structure and features of a creation myth. ☐
Green ⬤

NARRATIVE

Pandora's Box

Two brothers in Ancient Greece, named Epimetheus and Prometheus, had upset Zeus, King of the Gods, by giving the gift of fire to humans and now Zeus wanted to punish them.

He created a beautiful woman called Pandora and took her to Prometheus, but he refused to accept her because he knew Zeus wanted to punish him. Epimetheus thought Pandora was so beautiful that he fell in love with her, so he agreed to marry her.

One day the god Mercury arrived, carrying a magnificent box. He asked Epimetheus if he could leave the box with them until he returned from his journey. Mercury would not tell them what the box contained but only that it must never be opened.

Pandora had promised Mercury she would never open the box. But she could not forget about it. She began to imagine that it contained great treasures.

Eventually, Pandora's curiosity got the better of her and one day she grabbed the box, unfastened it and lifted the heavy lid. To her horror, there were no great treasures inside.

Instead, it was crammed with all the terrible evils of hate, despair and jealousy. They poured out like a swarm of bees. With a horrified cry, Pandora slammed the lid shut.

Then Pandora could hear a voice calling to her from the box, pleading with her to be let out. She did not want to be tricked again, and when Epimetheus, who had heard her cry, came into the room, she asked what she should do. He agreed that nothing inside the box could be worse than the evils that had already been released, so they cautiously opened the lid.

There at the bottom of the box was Hope. It fluttered from the box like a beautiful dragonfly and out into the world, so even though Pandora had released pain and suffering upon the world, she had also let the world have Hope.

Illustration © 2009, Simon Smith/Beehive Illustration.

PHOTOCOPIABLE **SCHOLASTIC**

NARRATIVE

Name	Date

A new hero (1)

■ Draw and label your hero.

Draw the hero.

hair:

face:

clothes:

weapons or tools:

What is my hero's name?
_____

Where does the hero live?
_____

strengths:
_____
_____

weaknesses:
_____
_____

I can identify the characteristics of heroes. ☐

Red ○
Amber ○
Green ○

NARRATIVE

UNIT 3 Stories from other cultures

Literacy objectives

Speak and listen for a wide range of purposes in different contexts
Strand 4 Drama
● Reflect on how working in role helps to explore complex issues.

Read and write for a range of purposes on paper and on screen
Strand 7 Understanding and interpreting texts
● Infer writers' perspectives from what is written and from what is implied.
● Compare different types of narrative and information texts and identify how they are structured.
Strand 8 Engaging with and responding to texts
● Reflect on reading habits and preferences and plan personal reading goals.
Strand 9 Creating and shaping texts
● Reflect independently and critically on their own writing and edit and improve it.
● Experiment with different narrative form and styles to write own stories.
● Vary the pace and develop the viewpoint through the use of direct and reported speech, portrayal of action and selection of detail.
Strand 10 Text structure and organisation
● Experiment with the order of sections and paragraphs to achieve different effects.
Strand 11 Sentence structure and punctuation
● Adapt sentence structure to different text-types, purposes and readers.
● Punctuate sentences accurately, including using speech marks and apostrophes.

Key aspects of learning

Evaluation
● As they read and compare the work of particular authors, children will express and justify their judgements about books and about the author's style.
Enquiry
● Children will decide how to answer questions about an author by using different sources of information, surveys of opinion and so on.
Creative thinking
● Children will work in role, developing ideas to deepen understanding of the text with which they are working.
Social skills
● Children will participate in an extended group activity. They will take on a clearly defined role in the group, negotiate with others and reach agreement.
Self-awareness
● Children will discuss and reflect on their personal responses to texts.
Communication
● Children will develop their ability to discuss as they work collaboratively in paired, group and whole-class contexts. They will communicate outcomes orally, in writing and through ICT if appropriate.

Assessment focuses

Reading
AF3 (deduce, infer or interpret information, events or ideas from texts).
AF5 (explain and comment on writers' use of language, including grammatical and literary features at word and sentence level).
AF6 (identify and comment on writers' purposes and viewpoints, and the overall effect of the text on the reader).
AF7 (relate texts to their social, cultural and historical contexts and literary traditions).

Writing
AF3 (organise and present whole texts effectively, sequencing and structuring information, ideas and events).

Speaking and listening
Drama (identify qualities of others' performance; explore complex issues through role play; sustain a role).

Resources

Phase 1 activities
Photocopiable page, 'Characters (versions 1 and 2)
Photocopiable page, 'Writing in role (versions 1 and 2)
Phase 2 activities
Interactive activity, 'Direct and reported speech'
Photocopiable page, 'Direct and reported speech'
Photocopiable page, 'Story planner' (versions 1 and 2)
Phase 3 activities
Interactive activity, 'Which text type?'
Interactive activity, 'Tortoise's trick'
Photocopiable page, 'The Tortoise tricks the Rabbit'
Recommended texts
'Spider's Web' from *Tales from Africa* retold by Kathleen Arnott (ISBN 978-0192-75079-2)
'Bre-nancy and the Thirteen Plantains' from *Stories from the Caribbean* by Petronella Breinburg (ISBN 978-0750-24952-2)
'Amul and the Drum' by Campbell Perry from *All New 100 Literacy Hours: Year 5* (ISBN 978-0439-94525-7)

Unit 3 ⬜ Stories from other cultures

Learning outcomes	Assessment opportunity and evidence	Assessment focuses (AFs)		Success criteria
		Level 2	**Level 3**	
Phase ① activities pages 53-54				
Characters • Children can identify similarities and differences between characters. • Children can identify use of language to create particular effects in narrative.	• Paired activity where children record the similarities and differences between main characters in three stories and give feedback of their preferences. • Children's written responses on the photocopiable page. Oral feedback with notes made against the class list.	**Reading AF3** • Simple, plausible inference about events and information, using evidence from text. • Comments based on textual cues, sometimes misunderstood. **Reading AF7** • General features of a few text types identified. • Some awareness that books are set in different times and places.	**Reading AF6** • Straightforward inference based on a single point of reference in the text. • Responses to text show meaning established at a literal level or based on personal speculation. **Reading AF7** • Some simple connections between texts identified. • Recognition of some features of the context of texts.	• I can find similarities and differences between characters. • I can identify use of language to create particular effects in narrative.
Writing in role Children can work in role and empathise with characters.	• Supported group activity where children discuss ideas and write a letter in the role of a character. • Oral responses and completed photocopiable page.	**Writing AF3** • Some basic sequencing of ideas or material. • Openings and/or closings sometimes signalled.	**Writing AF3** • Some attempt to organise ideas with related points placed next to each other. • Openings and closings usually signalled. • Some attempt to sequence ideas or material logically.	I can reflect on how working in role helps explore complex issues.
Phase ② activities pages 55-56				
Direct and reported speech Children can understand and use direct and reported speech.	• Independent activity where children identify direct and reported speech and describe how it conveys action, plot and adds detail. • Oral responses and completed interactive activity.	**Reading AF5** • Some effective language choices noted. • Some familiar patterns of language identified.	**Reading AF5** • A few basic features of writer's use of language identified, but with little or no comment.	• I can revise the punctuation of dialogue to convey an action and add detail. • I can understand the use of direct and reported speech.
Retell a story in the first person Children can write a version of a story from another character's point of view, told in the first person.	• Paired activity where children retell a story and compare their new version with the original. • Oral feedback, written responses on the photocopiable page and notes against the class list.	**Reading AF6** • Some awareness that writers have viewpoints and purposes. • Simple statements about likes and dislikes in reading, sometimes with reasons. **Writing AF3** • Some basic sequencing of ideas or material. • Openings and/or closings sometimes signalled.	**Reading AF6** • Comments identify main purpose. • Express personal response but with little awareness of writer's viewpoint or effect on reader. **Writing AF3** • Some attempt to organise ideas with related points placed next to each other. • Openings and closings usually signalled. • Some attempt to sequence ideas or material logically.	• I can compare written and oral versions. • I can retell a story in the first person.
Phase ③ activities pages 57-58				
Which text type? Children can write the same sentences in different text forms and identify changes to the structure.	• Paired activity where children identify which text form sentences come from and identify the language features used. • Children's completed interactive activity and oral responses.	**Reading AF5** • Some effective language choices noted. • Some familiar patterns of language identified.	**Reading AF5** • A few basic features of writer's use of language identified, but with little or no comment.	• I can identify different text types. • I can describe the features of different text types.

Unit 3 📖 Stories from other cultures

Learning outcomes	Assessment opportunity and evidence	Assessment focuses (AFs)		Success criteria
		Level 2	Level 3	
Re-ordering a paragraph Children can recognise the effects of ordering text.	● Paired activity where children listen to a story, re-order a first-person justification and discuss their outcomes. ● Children's discussions and completed interactive activities.	**Writing AF3** ● Some basic sequencing of ideas or material. ● Openings and/or closings sometimes signalled.	**Writing AF3** ● Some attempt to organise ideas with related points placed next to each other. ● Openings and closings usually signalled. ● Some attempt to sequence ideas or material logically.	I can experiment with the order of sections and paragraphs to achieve effects.

Learning outcomes	Assessment opportunity and evidence	Assessment focuses (AFs)		Success criteria
		Level 4	Level 5	

Phase ① activities pages 53-54

Characters ● Children can identify similarities and differences between characters. ● Children can identify use of language to create particular effects in narrative.	● Paired activity where children record the similarities and differences between main characters in three stories and give feedback of their preferences. ● Children's written responses on the photocopiable page. Oral feedback with notes made against the class list.	**Reading AF3** ● Comments make inferences based on evidence from different points in the text. ● Inferences often correct, but comments are not always rooted securely in the text or repeat narrative or content. **Reading AF7** ● Features common to different texts or versions of the same text identified, with simple comment. ● Simple comment on the effect that the reader's or writer's context has on the meaning of texts.	**Reading AF3** ● Comments develop explanation of inferred meanings drawing on evidence across the text. ● Comments make inferences and deductions based on textual evidence. **Reading AF7** ● Comments identify similarities and differences between texts, or versions, with some explanation. ● Some explanation of how the contexts in which texts are written and read contribute to meaning.	● I can find similarities and differences between characters. ● I can identify use of language to create particular effects in narrative.
Writing in role Children can work in role and empathise with characters.	● Group activity where children discuss ideas and write a letter in the role of a character. ● Oral responses and the completed photocopiable page.	**Writing AF3** ● Ideas organised by clustering related points or by time sequence. ● Ideas are organised simply with a fitting opening and closing, sometimes linked. ● Ideas or material generally in logical sequence but overall direction of writing not always clearly signalled.	**Writing AF3** ● Material is structured clearly, with sentences organised into appropriate paragraphs. ● Development of material is effectively managed across text. ● Overall direction of the text supported by clear links between paragraphs.	I can reflect on how working in role helps explore complex issues.

Phase ② activities pages 55-56

Direct and reported speech Children can understand and use direct and reported speech.	● Independent activity where children identify direct and reported speech and describe how it conveys action, plot and adds detail. ● Oral responses and the completed photocopiable page.	**Reading AF5** ● Some basic features of writer's use of language identified. ● Simple comments on writer's choices.	**Reading AF5** ● Various features of writer's use of language identified, with some explanation. ● Comments show some awareness of the effect of writer's language choices.	● I can revise the punctuation of dialogue to convey an action and add detail. ● I can understand the use of direct and reported speech.

Unit 3 📖 Stories from other cultures

Learning outcomes	Assessment opportunity and evidence	Assessment focuses (AFs)		Success criteria
		Level 4	Level 5	
Retell a story in the first person Children can write a version of a story from another character's point of view, told in the first person.	• Paired activity where children retell a story and compare their new version with the original. • Oral feedback, written responses on the photocopiable page and notes against the class list.	**Reading AF6** • Main purpose identified. • Simple comments show some awareness of writer's viewpoint. • Simple comment on overall effect on reader. **Writing AF3** • Ideas organised by clustering related points or by time sequence. • Ideas are organised simply with a fitting opening and closing, sometimes linked. • Ideas or material generally in logical sequence but overall direction of writing not always clearly signalled.	**Reading AF6** • Main purpose clearly identified, often through general overview. • Viewpoint in texts clearly identified, with some, often limited, explanation. • General awareness of effect on the reader, with some, often limited, explanation. **Writing AF3** • Material is structured clearly, with sentences organised into appropriate paragraphs. • Development of material is effectively managed across text. • Overall direction of the text supported by clear links between paragraphs.	• I can compare written and oral versions. • I can retell a story in the first person.

Phase ③ activities pages 57–58

Which text type? Children can write the same sentences in different text forms and identify changes to the structure.	• Independent activity where children identify which text form sentences come from and identify the language features used. • Children's completed interactive activity and oral responses.	**Reading AF5** • Some basic features of writer's use of language identified. • Simple comments on writer's choices.	**Reading AF5** • Various features of writer's use of language identified, with some explanation. • Comments show some awareness of the effect of writer's language choices.	• I can identify different text types. • I can describe the features of different text types.
Re-ordering a paragraph Children can recognise the effects of ordering text.	• Independent and paired activity where children read a story, re-order a first-person justification and discuss their outcomes. • Children's discussions and completed interactive activities.	**Writing AF3** • Ideas organised by clustering related points or by time sequence. • Ideas are organised simply with a fitting opening and closing, sometimes linked. • Ideas or material generally in logical sequence but overall direction of writing not always clearly signalled.	**Writing AF3** • Material is structured clearly, with sentences organised into appropriate paragraphs. • Development of material is effectively managed across text. • Overall direction of the text supported by clear links between paragraphs.	I can experiment with the order of sections and paragraphs to achieve effects.

Phase ① Characters

Learning outcomes
● Children can identify similarities and differences between characters.
● Children can identify use of language to create particular effects in narrative.

Success criteria
● I can find similarities and differences between characters.
● I can identify use of language to create particular effects in narrative.

Setting the context
This activity should be carried out once children have read and explored the key features of stories from other cultures in shared, guided and independent reading. They should have compared and contrasted typical characters, settings and plot structures, use of language and dialogue and purposes. They should understand that stories from other cultures usually originated through oral storytelling and have many of the features of traditional tales. Discuss the characters and how the author conveys them from three of the stories being studied in the course of this unit, for example, 'Spider's Web' from *Tales from Africa,* retold by Kathleen Arnott; 'Bre-nancy and the Thirteen Plantains' from *Stories from the Caribbean* by Petronella Breinburg; 'Amul and the Drum' by Campbell Perry; or from other stories being read. Arrange the children into pairs of similar ability. Provide them with the photocopiable page, 'Characters' (version 1 or 2) and ask them to compare the main characters from each story. You may also want to provide copies of the chosen tales for children to refer to while completing the photocopiable page. Children working at levels 2–3 can use version 1 of the photocopiable page.

Assessment opportunity
This activity provides the opportunity to assess children's ability to make inferences and deductions based on what is written and what is implied by the author. Observe pairs as they discuss and make notes of their contributions. Invite children to give oral feedback of their opinions to others and compare ideas.

Assessment evidence
At levels 2–3, children will make simple descriptions of the main character, mostly based on literal description in the text. For example: *Other characters think he is cunning.* At levels 4–5, children will make inferences about the characters based on their behaviour using evidence from different points in the text. For example: *They think he is playing a trick because they have seen him play tricks before.* Use notes of paired responses and the completed photocopiable pages to provide evidence for Reading AF3 and AF7.

Next steps
Support: Use the differentiated version of the photocopiable page 'Characters' with the children.
Extension: Invite children to write a character sketch of their preferred main character.

Key aspects of learning
Evaluation: As they read and compare the work of particular authors, children will express and justify their judgements about books and about the author's style.
Self-awareness: Children will discuss and reflect on their personal responses to texts.
Communication: Children will develop their ability to discuss as they work collaboratively in paired, group and whole-class contexts. They will communicate outcomes orally, in writing and through ICT if appropriate.

NARRATIVE

Phase ① Writing in role

Learning outcome
Children can work in role and empathise with characters.

Success criteria
I can reflect on how working in role helps explore complex issues.

Setting the context
This activity should be undertaken once children have explored the characteristics of the main characters in different stories from other cultures. Children should have had the opportunity to perform role play such as hot-seating and to ask and answer questions in the roles of the main characters from the stories in order to discover reasons for actions and behaviour. Explain that they are going to write a letter as the main character from one of the stories to justify and explain their actions. Invite children to work in small groups and to discuss ideas for the letter, making notes of their ideas. Children working at levels 2–3 can work with a supporting adult. Provide the children with the photocopiable page 'Writing in role' (version 1 or 2) and ask them to complete the letter, giving three reasons for or justifications of his/her behaviour. Children working at levels 2–3 will use version 1 of the photocopiable page.

Assessment opportunity
This activity provides the opportunity to observe how well children understand the character and can interpret what the author says and implies about him or her. A supporting adult can make notes of individual children's contributions to the group discussion prior to writing.

Assessment evidence
At levels 2–3, children will use simple connectives to organise their letter (such as 'but', 'so'), but their ideas are not always arranged in a sequential, logical order. At levels 4–5, children will use temporal connectives or cause and effect to link their paragraphs which are arranged in a logical sequence. Use children's oral responses and completed photocopiable pages to provide evidence for Writing AF3.

Next steps
Support: For children who struggled to write in role, give them more opportunities to be in the hot-seat in the role of the character prior to writing.
Extension: Invite children to write a response to the letter from another character's viewpoint.

Key aspects of learning
Evaluation: As they read and compare the work of particular authors, children will express and justify their judgements about books and about the author's style.
Creative thinking: Children will work in role, developing ideas to deepen understanding of the text with which they are working.
Self-awareness: Children will discuss and reflect on their personal responses to texts.
Communication: Children will develop their ability to discuss as they work collaboratively in paired, group and whole-class contexts. They will communicate outcomes orally, in writing and through ICT if appropriate.

Phase ② Direct and reported speech

Learning outcome
Children can understand and use direct and reported speech.

Success criteria
● I can revise the punctuation of dialogue to convey an action and add detail.
● I can understand the use of direct and reported speech.

Setting the context
This activity should be carried out after the children have explored the use of dialogue in stories in shared and guided reading and writing. They should have revised the rules for writing, punctuating and laying out dialogue. They should have explored how direct speech is used in stories to convey action and character and to move the plot along. Ask the children working at levels 2–3 to do the interactive activity 'Direct and reported speech', where they label examples of direct or reported speech. Children working at levels 4–5 identify the type of speech and change the direct speech to reported speech and vice versa on photocopiable page 'Direct and reported speech'.

Assessment opportunity
This activity provides the opportunity to assess whether children are secure in their understanding of direct and reported speech. When children have completed the activities, ask them to describe how the dialogue has been used to add extra information and convey action and plot. Ask them to say when and why they would use reported speech and direct speech in their own writing. Responses might include: varying the use of sentence structures to maintain readers' interest in fiction; direct speech can convey how the words are spoken through powerful speech verbs; reported speech is better suited to writing recounts and journalistic text. Make notes on the children's responses.

Assessment evidence
At levels 2–3 children will identify a few basic features in the sentences, for example, they may notice that speech marks are used in direct speech. At levels 4–5, children will be able to identify the use of direct and reported speech in sentences and will comment on the use of pronouns in reported speech and speech marks in reported speech. Use the completed interactive activities, and photocopiable page notes of their oral responses to provide evidence against Reading AF5.

Next steps
Support: Children who confuse direct and reported speech should be given the opportunity to revise the layout and conventions of speech punctuation.
Extension: Encourage children to change the direct speech in a passage from a story they have been reading and comment on the effect this has on the text.

Key aspects of learning
Evaluation: As they read and compare the work of particular authors, children will express and justify their judgements about books and about the author's style.
Self-awareness: Children will discuss and reflect on their personal responses to texts.
Communication: Children will develop their ability to discuss as they work collaboratively in paired, group and whole-class contexts. They will communicate outcomes orally, in writing and through ICT if appropriate.

NARRATIVE

Phase ② Retell a story in the first person

Learning outcome
Children can write a version of a story from another character's point of view, told in the first person.

Success criteria
● I can compare written and oral versions.
● I can retell a story in the first person.

Setting the context
This activity should be undertaken after the children have had the opportunity to explore and analyse narrative voice in stories from other cultures through shared and guided reading and writing. Children should have had the opportunity to retell stories through role-play activities, including hot-seating, using the first-person voice and taking other characters' points of view. Invite the children to choose one of the stories they have been reading in the unit and take turns to retell it to a partner from a different character's point of view. Tell them to use a clear beginning, middle and ending. Ask the children to write this new version of the story using the photocopiable page 'Story planner' (versions 1 or 2). Children working at levels 2–3 can collaborate with their partner to write the story using version 1 of the photocopiable page to record their ideas.

Assessment opportunity
This activity provides an opportunity to assess children's abilities to empathise with characters and see events from their point of view. When children have completed their retelling, invite them to describe how the story is different from the original version. Make notes of their responses.

Assessment evidence
At levels 2–3, children will show a clear beginning, middle and ending in their retellings and story plans. At levels 4–5, children will show clarity in the organisation of their ideas and show a link between the beginning and ending such as: 'and that is why...', with a reference to the opening sentence. Use your notes of children's oral responses and the completed photocopiable pages to provide evidence against Reading AF6 and Writing AF3.

Next steps
Support: For children who struggled to write in role, give them more opportunities to be in the hot-seat in the role of the character prior to writing.
Extension: Invite children to expand their stories into a fuller version.

Key aspects of learning
Evaluation: As they read and compare the work of particular authors, children will express and justify their judgements about books and about the author's style.
Creative thinking: Children will work in role, developing ideas to deepen understanding of the text with which they are working.
Self-awareness: Children will discuss and reflect on their personal responses to texts.
Communication: Children will develop their ability to discuss as they work collaboratively in paired, group and whole-class contexts. They will communicate outcomes orally, in writing and through ICT if appropriate.

Phase ③ Which text type?

Learning outcome
Children can write the same sentence in different text forms and identify changes to the structure.

Success criteria
● I can identify different text types.
● I can describe the features of different text types

Setting the context
This activity should be undertaken after the children have had the opportunity to explore the sentence structures of different text types including features of grammar and punctuation, verb tenses and uses of emotive and evocative language in shared and guided writing. They should have had the opportunity to change a sentence on a single subject to reflect the features of different types of text. Invite children to do the interactive activity 'Which text type?' to identify text-types, based on sentence structure. Children working at levels 2–3 should do the interactive activity with a partner.

Assessment opportunity
When children have completed the interactive activity, ask them to identify the language features that indicate the type of text the sentences belong to. Make notes of their responses.

Assessment evidence
At levels 2–3, children will mostly be able to explain their answers by referring to verb use. At levels 4–5, children will refer to verb tenses and other language features such as linking phrases, for example: 'Ever after', 'Long ago' and 'And that is why...'. Make notes of children's responses and use the completed interactive activity as evidence against Reading AF5.

Next steps
Support: For children who struggled to recognise the language features in the sentences, revise the typical features of different text types when the opportunity arises during the work in this unit.
Extension: Give the children a subject, for example a sport or a food, and invite children to write a sentence about it in five different text forms.

Key aspects of learning
Self-awareness: Children will discuss and reflect on their personal responses to texts.
Communication: Children will develop their ability to discuss as they work collaboratively in paired, group and whole-class contexts. They will communicate outcomes orally, in writing and through ICT if appropriate

NARRATIVE

Phase ③ Re-ordering a paragraph

Learning outcome
Children can recognise the effects of ordering text.

Success criteria
I can experiment with the order of sections and paragraphs to achieve effects.

Setting the context
This activity should be undertaken after the children have had the opportunity to experiment with the order of sentences and information within paragraphs in shared, guided and independent writing. They should be aware that the order of sentences and paragraphs can strengthen or weaken the desired effect on the reader. Ensure the children are familiar with the story 'The Tortoise tricks the Rabbit' before they begin the activity, by reading the story on the photocopiable page to them. Children working at levels 4-5 read the text independently. Explain that they are going to explore Tortoise's justification for playing the trick in the interactive activity 'Tortoise's trick'. They are to re-order the sentences to put Tortoise's point of view as forcefully as possible. Remind the children that putting positive ideas before negative ideas can influence the reader's thoughts about an issue.

Assessment opportunity
When children have re-ordered the paragraph, ask them to read the passage aloud in pairs and compare their answers. Ask them which order makes them feel the most sympathy with Tortoise and how the order affects their opinions. Make notes of the children's responses.

Assessment evidence
At levels 2-3, children will use the connectives 'but' and 'that' to help them order the sentences and will order some but not all the other sentences correctly. At levels 4-5, children will use the words and phrases 'but' and 'too' to help them choose the best sequence. They are aware that the sentence containing the word 'cruel' is a negative reference to Tortoise so use this sentence at the ending of the sequence. Use the completed interactive activity to provide evidence against Writing AF3.

Next steps
Support: Invite children to copy a paragraph of writing done earlier in the unit, cut it into sentence strips and ask them to experiment with the strips to create the best effect.
Extension: Invite children to write a response from Rabbit to counter Tortoise's justification, cut out the sentences and experiment with the order to create the best effect.

Key aspects of learning
Self-awareness: Children will discuss and reflect on their personal responses to texts.
Communication: Children will develop their ability to discuss as they work collaboratively in paired, group and whole-class contexts. They will communicate outcomes orally, in writing and through ICT if appropriate.

Periodic assessment

Reading

Learning outcomes
● Children can highlight similarities and differences between characters.
● Children can identify and explain key phrases.
● Children can reflect on reading habits and explore preferences.

Success criteria
● I can identify use of language to develop characters and create particular effects.
● I can review a story using evidence from the text.

Setting the context
Ensure children have read, researched and analysed the different stories. Review the work that has been done during the course of this unit and discuss children's achievements with them. Ask them what they found easy to accomplish and what was difficult. Invite children to choose one of the stories from the unit and give an oral review to the group or class, illustrating the features of the story with evidence from the text.

Assessment opportunity
This assessment provides the opportunity for children to evaluate their own understanding of the structure and features of stories from other cultures. The oral story review provides the opportunity to assess children's security in their learning across the unit. Make notes of their responses.

Assessment evidence
At levels 2-3, children's responses will contain basic information recalled from the story, with references to the setting and characters based on the written text. At levels 4-5, children will also refer to authorial voice and point of view. Use children's oral self-assessments and your notes to provide evidence against Reading AF2, AF6 and AF7.

Writing

Learning outcomes
● Children can edit and improve their writing.
● Children can use features of stories from other cultures, different authorial voices and direct and reported speech in their own writing.

Success criteria
● I can revise and edit my own writing to achieve a final version.
● I can write my own version of a story from another culture, from different characters' points of view.
● I can use direct and reported speech.

Setting the context
Collect the work that has been completed during the course of the unit and discuss individual children's achievements with them. Make notes of their responses. Ask children to choose a piece of writing done at the beginning of the unit. Ask them to swap with a partner. Tell them to read their partner's work and describe what they think is needed to polish it. Invite them to revise their own writing, taking account of what they have learned during the whole unit and their partner's comments.

Assessment opportunity
When children have completed their stories, they swap them with their partners again. Invite the partners to peer-evaluate what they have written. Assess children's abilities to evaluate their own or another's writing.

Assessment evidence
Children's oral responses and their partner's evaluations of their stories can be used as evidence against Writing AF1.

Name

Date

Writing in role (1)

Address

_____

_____

_____

Date

_____

Dear _____

It really wasn't my fault that

_____

_____

_____

Let me explain. Firstly,

_____

_____

Also,

_____

_____

Finally,

_____

_____

_____

From _____

Red
Amber
Green

I can reflect on how working in role helps explore complex issues. ◻

Name _____   Date _____

NARRATIVE

Story planner (1)

- Briefly retell the story from another character's point of view using 'I', the first-person voice.
- What is the name of your character?

Story opening Who? (characters) Where? (setting) What? (plot)		
Middle Who? What? Where? Why?		
Story ending		

I can compare written and oral versions. ☐
I can retell a story in the first person. ☐

Red ○
Amber ○
Green ○

NARRATIVE
UNIT 4 Older literature

Literacy objectives

Speak and listen for a wide range of purposes in different contexts
Strand 2 Listening and responding
- Identify some aspects of talk that vary between formal and informal occasions.

Read and write for a range of purposes on paper and on screen
Strand 8 Engaging with and responding to texts
- Reflect on reading habits and preferences and plan personal reading goals.
Strand 9 Creating and shaping texts
- Reflect independently and critically on their own writing and edit and improve it.
- Adapt non-narrative forms and styles to write fiction or factual texts, including poems.
- Vary the pace and develop the viewpoint through the use of direct and reported speech, portrayal of action and selection of detail.
Strand 10 Text structure and organisation
- Experiment with the order of sections and paragraphs to achieve different effects.
Strand 11 Sentence structure and punctuation
- Punctuate sentences accurately, including using speech marks and apostrophes.

Key aspects of learning

Evaluation
- As they read and compare the work of particular authors, children will express and justify their judgements about books and about the author's style.
Self-awareness
- Children will discuss and reflect on their personal responses to the texts.
Communication
- Children will develop their ability to discuss as they work collaboratively in paired, group and whole-class contexts. They will communicate outcomes orally, in writing and through ICT if appropriate.

Assessment focuses

Reading
AF3 *(deduce, infer or interpret information, events or ideas from texts).*
AF7 *(relate texts to their social, cultural and historical contexts and literary traditions).*

Writing
AF2 *(produce texts which are appropriate to task, reader and purpose).*
AF5 *(vary sentences for clarity, purpose and effect).*

Speaking and listening
Listening and responding (understand difference between informal and formal speech).

Resources

Phase 1 activities
Photocopiable page, 'The Water Babies (a)'
Photocopiable page, 'The Impractical Chimney-Sweep (a)'
Photocopiable page, 'Comparing two stories',
Interactive activity, 'Comparing two stories',
Photocopiable page, 'The Impractical Chimney-Sweep (b)'
Phase 2 activities
Photocopiable page, 'The Water Babies (b)'
Phase 3 activities
Photocopiable page, 'The Water Babies (a)'
Photocopiable page, 'The Impractical Chimney-Sweep (b)
Periodic assessment
Photocopiable page, 'Narrative 4 Reading assessment'
Photocopiable page, 'Narrative 4 Writing assessment'
Recommended texts
The Water Babies by Charles Kingsley (ISBN 978-1841-35236-7)
The Impractical Chimney-Sweep by Rosemary Anne Sisson (ASIN B0017YK1MK)

Unit 4 ▭ Older literature

Learning outcomes	Assessment opportunity and evidence	Assessment focuses (AFs)		Success criteria
		Level 2	Level 3	
Phase ① activity page 66				
Chimney-sweeps • Children can understand how characters are introduced. • Children can use a grid to compare the times represented in two stories.	• Independent activity where children read and compare extracts from two stories written at an earlier time and complete an interactive activity. • Oral feedback and completed interactive activities.	**Reading AF3** • Simple, plausible inference about events and information, using evidence from text. • Comments based on textual cues, sometimes misunderstood. **Reading AF7** • General features of a few text types identified. • Some awareness that books are set in different times and places.	**Reading AF3** • Straightforward inference based on a single point of reference in the text. • Responses to text show meaning established at a literal level or based on personal speculation. **Reading AF7** • Some simple connections between texts identified. • Recognition of some features of the context of texts.	• I can compare stories written at an earlier time. • I can identify how characters are introduced.
Phase ② activity page 67				
Direct and reported speech Children can apply skills of direct and reported speech in writing.	• Independent activity where children rewrite a dialogue as reported speech and evaluate the effect on the text. • Children's written outcomes and oral feedback.	**Writing AF2** • Some basic purpose established. • Some appropriate features of the given form used. • Some attempts to adopt appropriate style.	**Writing AF2** • Purpose established at a general level. • Main features of selected form sometimes signalled to the reader. • Some attempts at appropriate style, with attention to reader.	I can vary pace and develop viewpoint through the use of direct and reported speech in writing.
Phase ③ activity page 68				
Write in an author's style Children can write a scene in a style similar to that of an author.	• Supported group activity where children discuss an author's style and write in the same style. • Children's oral discussions and written outcomes.	**Writing AF5** • Some variation in sentence openings. • Mainly simple sentences with and used to connect clauses. • Past and present tense generally consistent.	**Writing AF5** • Reliance mainly on simply structured sentences, variation with support. • and, but, so are the most common connectives, subordination occasionally. • Some limited variation in use of tense and verb forms, not always secure.	• I can collect and identify features of an author's style. • I can write in the style of an author.

Unit 4 Older literature

Learning outcomes	Assessment opportunity and evidence	Assessment focuses (AFs)		Success criteria
		Level 4	Level 5	
Phase ① activity page 66				
Chimney-sweeps • Children can understand how characters are introduced. • Children can use a grid to compare the times represented in two stories.	• Independent activity where children read and compare extracts from two stories written at an earlier time and complete an interactive activity. • Oral feedback and written work on the photocopiable page.	**Reading AF3** • Comments make inferences based on evidence from different points in the text. • Inferences often correct, but comments are not always rooted securely in the text or repeat narrative or content. **Reading AF7** • Features common to different texts or versions of the same text identified, with simple comment. • Simple comment on the effect that the reader's or writer's context has on the meaning of texts.	**Reading AF3** • Comments develop explanation of inferred meanings drawing on evidence across the text. • Comments make inferences and deductions based on textual evidence. **Reading AF7** • Comments identify similarities and differences between texts, or versions, with some explanation. • Some explanation of how the contexts in which texts are written and read contribute to meaning.	• I can compare stories written at an earlier time. • I can identify how characters are introduced.
Phase ② activity page 67				
Direct and reported speech Children can apply skills of direct and reported speech in writing.	• Independent activity where children rewrite a dialogue as reported speech and evaluate the effect on the text. • Children's written outcomes and oral feedback.	**Writing AF2** • Main purpose of writing is clear but not always consistently maintained. • Main features of selected form are clear and appropriate to purpose. • Style generally appropriate to task, though awareness of reader not always sustained.	**Writing AF2** • Main purpose of writing is clear and consistently maintained. • Features of selected form clearly established with some adaptation to purpose. • Appropriate style clearly established to maintain reader's interest throughout.	I can vary pace and develop viewpoint through the use of direct and reported speech in writing.
Phase ③ activity page 68				
Write in an author's style Children can write a scene in a style similar to that of an author.	• Independent and group activity where children discuss an author's style and write in the same style. • Children's oral discussions and written outcomes.	**Writing AF5** • Some variety in length, structure or subject of sentences. • Use of some subordinating connectives, throughout the text. • Some variation, generally accurate, in tense and verb forms.	**Writing AF5** • A variety of sentence lengths, structures and subjects provides clarity and emphasis. • Wider range of connectives used to clarify relationship between ideas. • Some features of sentence structure used to build up detail or convey shades of meaning.	• I can collect and identify features of an author's style. • I can write in the style of an author.

NARRATIVE

Phase ① Chimney-sweeps

Learning outcomes
- Children can understand how characters are introduced.
- Children can use a grid to compare the times represented in two stories.

Success criteria
- I can compare stories written at an earlier time.
- I can identify how characters are introduced.

Setting the context
This activity should be carried out once children have read and explored stories written by authors from an earlier time. They should have compared use of language, punctuation, dialogue, settings and characters in shared and guided reading, and if possible listened to a class novel to familiarise themselves with the language and characterisation that feature in older literature. Read the two extracts to the children from the photocopiable pages, 'The Water Babies (a)' (written by Charles Kingsley in 1863) and 'The Impractical Chimney-Sweep (a)' (by Rosemary Anne Sisson, written in 1956). Explain a little about both stories; for example, both are about young boys who are chimney-sweeps but one was written at the time when children were used as chimney-sweeps and the other much later. (However, do not tell them which is which.) Provide children with their own copies to refer to. Ask the children to complete the photocopiable page 'Comparing two stories' to compare how the characters are introduced in both extracts and the type of language used by the authors. Alternatively, children working at levels 2–3 could do the interactive activity 'Comparing two stories'.

Assessment opportunity
When children have completed the photocopiable page or the interactive activity, invite them to expand their answers to show they can understand the differences in the way the authors have introduced the characters and recognise the way their use of language differs. Ask questions to draw out and deepen children's responses, for example: *Which story gives you more detail about the character? Why do you think that is? In* The Impractical Chimney-Sweep, *how do you think the author might tell you more about John William? Which do you find easier to read and why?*

Assessment evidence
At levels 2–3, children will make comments about preferences based on ease of reading. At levels 4–5, children will identify the more complex sentence structures as being from an earlier period of time. Use children's completed interactive activity, photocopiable page and oral responses to provide evidence against Reading AF3 and AF7.

Next steps
Support: Provide children with a further character description from *The Impractical Chimney-Sweep* using the extract on the photocopiable page 'The Impractical Chimney-Sweep (b)' and ask them to describe the way the character of John William's mother is introduced.
Extension: Invite children to write a character description of Tom from *The Water Babies* using modern vocabulary and sentence structures.

Key aspects of learning
Evaluation: As they read and compare the work of particular authors, children will express and justify their judgements about books and about the author's style.
Self-awareness: Children will discuss and reflect on their personal responses to the texts.
Communication: Children will develop their ability to discuss as they work collaboratively in paired, group and whole-class contexts. They will communicate outcomes orally, in writing and through ICT if appropriate.

NARRATIVE

Phase ② Direct and reported speech

Learning outcome
Children can apply skills of direct and reported speech in writing.

Success criteria
I can vary pace and develop viewpoint through the use of direct and reported speech in writing.

Setting the context
This activity should be undertaken once children have explored how an author's use of both direct and reported speech can affect the pace of a story. They should have investigated how the 'voice' and personality of characters can be conveyed to readers by use of powerful verbs and adverbs and how this varies between both types of speech. They should have discussed how dialogue moves the plot along. Ask the children to say why an author uses reported speech instead of direct speech. *Does it slow down the story or move it along? When would you use reported speech in your own fiction writing?* Provide the children with photocopiable page 'The Water Babies (b)' which is the second extract from *The Water Babies* by Charles Kingsley. Ask them to rewrite the dialogue between Mr Grimes and the Irish woman as reported speech and then re-read the extract to see the difference this makes.

Assessment opportunity
Ask children to read the extract aloud, including the change to reported speech. Ask them to explain how they think it affects the passage. *Does it give you as much interest as the original? Why? Why not? How does it affect the pace and rhythm of the writing? Which version do you prefer and why?* For children working at levels 2–3, ask them to explain how they changed the punctuation from the original direct speech to reported speech. Make notes of the children's oral responses.

Assessment evidence
At levels 2–3, children will mostly use accurate speech punctuation, and simple speech verbs in reporting clauses. At levels 4–5 children will vary the verbs in reporting clauses. They may suggest that using direct speech slows down the narrative. Use children's oral responses and written passages of reported speech to provide evidence against Writing AF2.

Next steps
Support: Provide further opportunities for changing direct speech to reported speech during the work in this unit.
Extension: Invite children to rewrite the reported speech at the end of the extract as direct speech using their imaginations.

Key aspects of learning
Evaluation: As they read and compare the work of particular authors, children will express and justify their judgements about books and about the author's style.
Self-awareness: Children will discuss and reflect on their personal responses to the texts.
Communication: Children will develop their ability to discuss as they work collaboratively in paired, group and whole-class contexts. They will communicate outcomes orally, in writing and through ICT if appropriate.

NARRATIVE

Phase ③ Write in an author's style

Learning outcome
Children can write a scene in a style similar to that of an author.

Success criteria
● I can collect and identify features of an author's style.
● I can write in the style of an author.

Setting the context
This activity should be undertaken after the children have discussed the style of writing by authors of older literature during shared and guided reading and in the class novel. They should have explored use of vocabulary, sentence structures and punctuation, and compared them with those used by modern authors writing in the same genres. Provide the children with copies of the text extracts on photocopiable pages 'The Water Babies (a)' and 'The Impractical Chimney-Sweep (b)'. Enlarge the first extract on the photocopiable page or display it on screen. Discuss with the children how the author uses long complex sentences with clauses separated by commas and semi-colons, but breaks up the passage with a short sentence 'He cried half his life and laughed the other half.' Ask them what effect the short sentence has. *Does it indicate a change of focus in the passage? Does it give this statement about Tom more impact?* Display an enlarged copy of the extract from *The Impractical Chimney-Sweep* on the photocopiable page or on screen. Identify the long sentences with clauses and phrases separated by commas. Look at the last sentence 'But she was different – and so was John William.' Invite the children to write a paragraph which describes a child chimney-sweep getting up in the morning before having to go out sweeping chimneys, using what they have learnt from the extracts and their own imaginations, and using sentence structures similar to the two authors.

Assessment opportunity
Children working at levels 2-3 should work in small groups with a supporting adult to build complex sentences using correct punctuation. Children working at levels 4-5 can write a paragraph independently.

Assessment evidence
At levels 2-3, children will tend to use the conjunctions 'and', 'but' or 'so' in their sentences. At levels 4-5, children will vary their sentence openings by occasional use of subordinating connectives such as 'Although…' or 'Meanwhile…'. Use children's oral responses during discussion and written outcomes to provide evidence against Writing AF5.

Next steps
Support: Invite children, during guided reading, to identify where longer complex sentences and short sentences have been used to vary pace and change focus.
Extension: Invite children to analyse the extracts written by Charles Kingsley and identify why the author uses semi-colons rather than commas.

Key aspects of learning
Evaluation: As they read and compare the work of particular authors, children will express and justify their judgements about books and about the author's style.
Self-awareness: Children will discuss and reflect on their personal responses to the texts.
Communication: Children will develop their ability to discuss as they work collaboratively in paired, group and whole-class contexts. They will communicate outcomes orally, in writing and through ICT if appropriate.

Periodic assessment

Reading

Learning outcomes
- Children can understand how characters are introduced.
- Children can identify aspects of writing that vary between formal and informal.

Success criteria
- I can understand how characters are introduced.
- I can identify formal and informal writing styles.
- I can recognise vocabulary from older literature.

Setting the context
This assessment should be carried out once children have completed Narrative Unit 4. Ensure that children have experienced reading and analysing the language and features of stories. Display the success criteria in the classroom. Review the work that has been done during the course of this unit and discuss children's achievements with them. Ask them what they found easy to accomplish and what was difficult. Make notes of their responses. Invite the children to demonstrate their understanding of the main story that has been shared during the course of the unit by completing the photocopiable page 'Narrative 4 Reading assessment'.

Assessment opportunity
This assessment provides the opportunity to evaluate children's understanding of how literature, which is set in a different period of time, is influenced by the period in which it was written or set. Go through children's responses orally to allow them to deepen and justify their answers to the questions, making notes.

Assessment evidence
At levels 2–3 children's responses to the questions will contain basic information recalled from the story. At levels 4–5, children's responses may contain appropriate references to the whole text that back up their answers. The answers and your observational notes will provide evidence against Reading AF2, AF5, AF6 and AF7.

Periodic assessment

Writing

Learning outcome
Children can draft an historical newspaper report.

Success criteria
I can plan and use non-narrative forms to write fiction or factual texts.

Setting the context
This assessment should be carried out once children have completed Narrative Unit 4. Collect the work that has been completed during the course of the unit and discuss individual children's achievements with them. Ask them to suggest what they found difficult about the writing in the unit and what they found easy to accomplish. Make notes of their responses. Ask children to choose an incident or scene from the main story shared during the unit. Ask them to imagine what a newspaper report from the period when the story is set would be like. *How might the language and vocabulary be different from today? Would they have used photographs or artists' impressions? How might the headline be different from today's newspapers?* Invite the children to work with a partner and make notes on the photocopiable page ' Narrative 4 Writing assessment' for a newspaper report.

Assessment opportunity
When children have finished planning their newspaper report with a partner, ask them to swap with another pair of children. Invite the partners to evaluate what the other pair has planned. This activity provides an opportunity to assess children's abilities to evaluate their own or another's writing against the agreed success criteria. Ask the partners to find two examples of their ideas that work well and one that needs developing and improvement. Once the children have drafted their report ask them how easy or difficult they found writing a newspaper report in the period of the story.

Assessment evidence
Judge the children's self- and peer-assessment comments against your own assessment and act on this accordingly. Provide constructive comments and small manageable targets for all children to move their work on during the next narrative unit. Children's oral responses of their own achievements and their partner's evaluations of their planned newspaper reports can be used to provide evidence against all Writing AFs but especially AF2.

Name	Date

Comparing two stories

	The Water Babies	The Impractical Chimney-Sweep
Which story describes the chimney-sweep's character?		
Which story opens by introducing the character?		
How was life similar for both chimney-sweeps?		
How was life different for both chimney-sweeps?		
Which story do you think was written first?		
Write a reason for your answer.		
Write words or phrases from each story that tell you they are set in the past.		
Which story uses complex punctuation?		
Write two complex punctuation marks.		

Red
Amber
Green

I can compare stories written at an earlier time. ☐

I can identify how characters are introduced. ☐

The Water Babies (b)

Soon they came up with a poor Irishwoman, trudging along with a bundle at her back. She had a gray shawl over her head, and a crimson madder petticoat; so you may be sure she came from Galway. She had neither shoes nor stockings, and limped along as if she were tired and footsore: but she was a very tall handsome woman, with bright gray eyes, and heavy black hair hanging about her cheeks. And she took Mr Grimes's fancy so much, that when he came alongside he called out to her:

"This is a hard road for a gradely foot like that. Will ye up, lass, and ride behind me?"

But, perhaps, she did not admire Mr Grimes's look and voice; for she answered quietly:

"No, thank you; I'd sooner walk with your little lad here."

"You may please yourself," growled Grimes, and went on smoking.

So she walked beside Tom, and talked to him, and asked him where he lived, and what he knew, and all about himself, till Tom thought he had never met such a pleasant-spoken woman. And she asked him, at last, whether he said his prayers; and seemed sad when he told her that he knew no prayers to say.

Then he asked her where she lived; and she said far away by the sea. And Tom asked her about the sea; and she told him how it rolled and roared over the rocks in winter nights, and lay still in the bright summer days for the children to bathe and play in it; and many a story more, till Tom longed to go and see the sea, and bathe in it likewise.

Illustration © 2009, Simon Smith/Beehive Illustration.

NARRATIVE

Name

Date

Narrative 4 Writing assessment

Write your headlines:

Illustration:

Write your report:

Continue and end your report:

I can plan and use non-narrative forms to write fiction or factual texts.

Red

Amber

Green

NARRATIVE
UNIT 5 Film narrative

Literacy objectives

Speak and listen for a wide range of purposes in different contexts
Strand 1 Speaking
- Tell a story using notes designed to cue techniques, such as repetition, recap and humour.

Strand 4 Drama
- Reflect on how working in role helps to explore complex issues.

Read and write for a range of purposes on paper and on screen
Strand 7 Understanding and interpreting texts
- Infer writers' perspectives from what is written and from what is implied.
- Compare different types of narrative and information texts and identify how they are structured.

Strand 8 Engaging and responding to texts
- Compare the usefulness of techniques such as visualisation, prediction and empathy in exploring the meaning of texts.
- Compare how a common theme is presented in poetry, prose and other media.

Strand 9 Creating and shaping texts
- Reflect independently and critically on their own writing and edit and improve it.
- Experiment with different narrative form and styles to write their own stories.

Strand 11 Sentence structure and punctuation
- Adapt sentence construction to different text-types, purposes and readers.
- Punctuate sentences accurately, including using speech marks and apostrophes.

Strand 12 Presentation
- Use a range of ICT programs to present texts, making informed choices about which electronic tools to use for different purposes.

Key aspects of learning

Enquiry
- Children will investigate and ask questions of film to develop their understanding. They will plan and present their own interpretations of film using different modes of communication.

Creative thinking
- Children will generate and extend imaginative ideas, to respond to and interpret ideas. They will suggest hypotheses, responding imaginatively through drama and talk, making connections and understanding relationships to create a written outcome.

Information processing
- Children will identify relevant information and explore patterns from a range of modes and use this to write their own versions of a visual text.

Reasoning
- Children will draw inferences and make deductions to clarify, extend and follow up ideas and conclusions in their oral and written work.

Key aspects of learning (contd)

Evaluation
● Children will present information orally, through drama and in writing. They will make judgements and justify their views and opinions, drawing on sources to support their evaluations. Children will discuss success criteria, give feedback to others and judge the effectiveness of their own work.

Communication
● Children will develop their skills to reflect critically on what they have seen. They will develop their ability to present a narrative through drama, orally and in writing and reflect critically on their own and others' work.

Empathy
● In discussing writing and working in role, children will develop their skills to recognise and understand the perspectives of other people. They will develop their ability to identify triggers or causes of other people's emotions and actions.

Assessment focuses

Reading
AF2 (understand, describe, select or retrieve information, events or ideas from texts and use quotation and reference to text).
AF3 (deduce, infer or interpret information, events or ideas from texts).
AF6 (identify and comment on writers' purposes and viewpoints, and the overall effect of the text on the reader).

Writing
AF1 (write imaginative, interesting and thoughtful texts).

Speaking and listening
Speaking (present ideas clearly using standard English).
Drama (improvise and sustain a role; work with others in performance).

Resources

Phase 1 activities
Video, *The Piano* by Aidan Gibbons
Interactive activity, 'Sequence of events'
Photocopiable page, 'Film order'
Phase 2 activities
Photocopiable page, 'Film flashback' (versions 1 and 2)
Periodic assessment
Photocopiable page, 'Narrative 5 Reading assessment'
Photocopiable page, 'Narrative 5 Writing assessment'

Unit 5 ☐ Film narrative

Learning outcomes	Assessment opportunity and evidence	Assessment focuses (AFs)		Success criteria
		Level 2	Level 3	
Phase ① activity page 78				
Narrative sequence • Children can form opinions and use textual evidence from a film to support and justify responses. • Children demonstrate that they can infer authors' perspectives.	• Independent activity where children sequence the events of a film and discuss narrative order and the effect of changing it. • Children's oral responses and completed interactive activity.	**Reading AF2** • Some specific, straightforward information recalled. • Generally clear idea of where to look for information. **Reading AF3** • Simple, plausible inference about events and information, using evidence from text. • Comments based on textual cues, sometimes misunderstood. **Reading AF6** • Some awareness that writers have viewpoints and purposes. • Simple statements about likes and dislikes in reading, sometimes with reasons.	**Reading AF2** • Simple, most obvious points identified though there may also be some misunderstanding. • Some comments include quotations from or references to text, but not always relevant. **Reading AF3** • Straightforward inference based on a single point of reference in the text. • Responses to text show meaning established at a literal level or based on personal speculation. **Reading AF6** • Comments identify main purpose. • Express personal response but with little awareness of writer's viewpoint or effect on reader.	I can explain why a film maker has chosen to arrange scenes in a certain order.
Phase ② activity page 79				
Writing dialogue • Children demonstrate that they can use speech punctuation accurately. • Children can reflect on how working in role helps to explore some of the complex issues within a film.	• Paired activity where children role play a conversation based on images and add dialogue for each scene. • Children's oral feedback and written outcomes on the photocopiable page.	**Writing AF1** • Mostly relevant ideas and content, sometimes repetitive or sparse. • Some apt word choices create interest. • Brief comments, questions about events or actions suggest viewpoint.	**Writing AF1** • Some appropriate ideas and content included. • Some attempt to elaborate on basic information or events. • Attempt to adopt viewpoint, though often not maintained or inconsistent.	I can write dialogue for a flashback.
Phase ③ activity page 80				
Flashback • Children demonstrate that they can manipulate narrative structure. • Children can reflect on their own writing and edit and improve it.	• Supported group activity where children role play planned flashback scenes, evaluate them, re-write their plans and perform their scenes. • Children's oral feedback and edited flashback plans.	**Writing AF1** • Mostly relevant ideas and content, sometimes repetitive or sparse. • Some apt word choices create interest. • Brief comments, questions about events or actions suggest viewpoint.	**Writing AF1** • Some appropriate ideas and content included. • Some attempt to elaborate on basic information or events. • Attempt to adopt viewpoint, though often not maintained or inconsistent.	• I can plan and write a flashback scene. • I can edit and improve my own writing.

Unit 5 ▢ Film narrative

Learning outcomes	Assessment opportunity and evidence	Assessment focuses (AFs)		Success criteria
		Level 4	Level 5	
Phase ① activity page 78				
Narrative sequence ● Children can form opinions and use textual evidence from a film to support and justify responses. ● Children demonstrate that they can infer authors' perspectives.	● Independent activity where children sequence the events of a film and discuss narrative order and the effect of changing it. ● Children's oral responses and completed interactive activity.	**Reading AF2** ● Some relevant points identified. ● Comments supported by some generally relevant textual reference or quotation. **Reading AF3** ● Comments make inferences based on evidence from different points in the text. ● Inferences often correct, but comments are not always rooted securely in the text or repeat narrative or content. **Reading AF6** ● Main purpose identified. ● Simple comments show some awareness of writer's viewpoint. ● Simple comment on overall effect on reader.	**Reading AF2** ● Most relevant points clearly identified, including those selected from different places in the text. ● Comments generally supported by relevant textual reference or quotation, even when points made are not always accurate. **Reading AF3** ● Comments develop explanation of inferred meanings drawing on evidence across the text. ● Comments make inferences and deductions based on textual evidence. **Reading AF6** ● Main purpose clearly identified, often through general overview. ● Viewpoint in texts clearly identified, with some, often limited, explanation. ● General awareness of effect on the reader, with some, often limited, explanation.	I can explain why a film maker has chosen to arrange scenes in a certain order.
Phase ② activity page 79				
Writing dialogue ● Children demonstrate that they can use speech punctuation accurately. ● Children can reflect on how working in role helps to explore some of the complex issues within a film.	● Independent and paired activity where children role play a conversation based on images and add dialogue for each scene. ● Children's oral feedback and written outcomes on the photocopiable page.	**Writing AF1** ● Relevant ideas and content chosen. ● Some ideas and material developed in detail. ● Straightforward viewpoint generally established and maintained.	**Writing AF 1** ● Relevant ideas and material developed with some imaginative detail. ● Development of ideas and material appropriately shaped for selected form. ● Clear viewpoint. established, generally consistent, with some elaboration.	I can write dialogue for a flashback.
Phase ③ activity page 80				
Flashback ● Children demonstrate that they can manipulate narrative structure. ● Children can reflect on their own writing and edit and improve it.	● Paired activity where children role play planned flashback scenes, evaluate them, re-write their plans and perform their scenes. ● Children's oral feedback and edited flashback plans.	**Writing AF1** ● Relevant ideas and content chosen. ● Some ideas and material developed in detail. ● Straightforward viewpoint generally established and maintained.	**Writing AF1** ● Relevant ideas and material developed with some imaginative detail. ● Development of ideas and material appropriately shaped for selected form. ● Clear viewpoint established, generally consistent, with some elaboration.	● I can plan and write a flashback scene. ● I can edit and improve my own writing.

Phase ① Narrative sequence

Learning outcomes
- Children can form opinions and use textual evidence from a film to support and justify responses.
- Children demonstrate that they can infer authors' perspectives.

Success criteria
I can explain why a film maker has chosen to arrange scenes in a certain order.

Setting the context
This activity should be carried out once children have watched and explored the film *The Piano* by Aidan Gibbons, from the CD-ROM. They should have noted their initial impressions and generated words to describe the theme and atmosphere of the film in shared and guided writing sessions. Invite the children to use the interactive activity 'Sequence of events' to demonstrate their understanding and recall of the events portrayed in the film. Ask children working at levels 4-5 to sequence the events in 'real' time, ie when they actually occurred. Children working at levels 2-3 should sequence the events as they occur in the film itself.

Assessment opportunity
When children have completed the interactive activity, invite them to suggest why they think the film maker arranged the elderly man's memories in this order. *How would the film be different if another order was used? Would it have the same effect on viewers? Why? Why not?* Make notes of the children's responses.

Assessment evidence
At levels 2-3, children will sequence the scenes from the film as they saw them happen. At levels 4-5, children will begin the sequence with the image of the old-fashioned boy followed by the scene of the man helping his friend. Use children's completed interactive activity and oral responses (explaining why the film maker might have arranged the scenes in the order they appear in the film) to provide evidence against Reading AF2, AF3 and AF6.

Next steps
Support: Provide children with a copy of the photocopiable page 'Film order' and ask them to sequence the events from the film as a group.
Extension: Invite children to write a narrative description of the events in the film, using the first person, from the man's viewpoint.

Key aspects of learning
Enquiry: Children will investigate and ask questions of film to develop their understanding. They will plan and present their own interpretations of film using different modes of communication.
Information processing: Children will identify relevant information and explore patterns from a range of modes and use this to write their own versions of a visual text.
Reasoning: Children will draw inferences and make deductions to clarify, extend and follow up ideas and conclusions in their oral and written work.
Communication: Children will develop their skills to reflect critically on what they have seen. They will develop their ability to present a narrative through drama, orally and in writing and reflect critically on their own and others' work.
Empathy: In discussing writing and working in role, children will develop their skills to recognise and understand the perspectives of other people. They will develop their ability to identify triggers or causes of other people's emotions and actions.

▲SCHOLASTIC

Phase ② Writing dialogue

Learning outcomes
● Children demonstrate that they can use speech punctuation accurately.
● Children can reflect on how working in role helps to explore some of the complex issues within a film.

Success criteria
I can write dialogue for a flashback.

Setting the context
This activity should be undertaken once children have studied and analysed the film *The Piano* by Aidan Gibbons from the CD-ROM. They should have taken part in role play conversations based on the characters in the film and had the opportunity to recreate their role play in written dialogue. Provide children with copies of the photocopiable page 'Film flashback' (versions 1 and 2) with three different scenes reflecting a theme similar to that of the film. Display the success criteria in the classroom. Discuss the images before commencing the activity and ask the children to suggest what is happening, who is featured, and when and where it takes place. Invite the children to work with a partner and role play a conversation for each scene on the page. Ask the children independently to write a short dialogue in the space beside each scene. Children working at levels 2–3 can use version 1, working in pairs to create a dialogue in speech bubbles.

Assessment opportunity
This activity provides the opportunity to assess whether children are able to transfer their learning and understanding of the work done on theme, character and dialogue in *The Piano* to different characters and settings. When children have completed the photocopiable page 'Film flashback', invite them to discuss their responses orally and give reasons for their choice of dialogue for each of the three scenes on the page. Make notes of their oral responses.

Assessment evidence
Children working at levels 2–3 write a simple dialogue using speech bubbles, showing a literal response to the images such as 'I am pleased the painting has been sold'. Children working at levels 4–5 demonstrate that they recognise the flashback part of the sequence of images by the use of 'memory' in their written dialogue. Use children's oral responses and written photocopiable pages to provide evidence against Writing AF1 (see also AF6).

Next steps
Support: Working with a supporting adult, children rewrite their speech bubbles as dialogue using speech punctuation.
Extension: Invite children to write a short film script using the scenes from the photocopiable page 'Film flashback'.

Key aspects of learning
Enquiry: Children will investigate and ask questions of film to develop their understanding. They will plan and present their own interpretations of film using different modes of communication.
Creative thinking: Children will generate and extend imaginative ideas, to respond to and interpret ideas. They will suggest hypotheses, responding imaginatively through drama and talk, making connections and understanding relationships to create a written outcome.
Information processing: Children will identify relevant information from a range of modes and use this to write their own versions of a visual text.
Reasoning: Children will draw inferences and make deductions to clarify, extend and follow up ideas and conclusions in their oral and written work.
Communication: Children will develop their skills to reflect critically on what they have seen. They will develop their ability to present a narrative through drama, orally and in writing and reflect critically on their own and others' work.
Empathy: In discussing writing and working in role, children will develop their skills to recognise and understand the perspectives of other people. They will develop their ability to identify triggers or causes of other people's emotions and actions.

NARRATIVE

Phase ③ Flashback

Learning outcomes
- Children demonstrate that they can manipulate narrative structure.
- Children can reflect on their own writing and edit and improve it.

Success criteria
- I can plan and write a flashback scene.
- I can edit and improve my own writing.

Setting the context
This assessment should be undertaken after the children have explored and analysed the film *The Piano* by Aidan Gibbons from the CD-ROM. They should have planned a character for a flashback scene in a story, based on their analysis of the theme and atmosphere in the film, using a graphic organiser or storyboard. Ask the children to work with a partner using both of their flashback plans. Ask them to role play each other's flashback scenes and evaluate their effectiveness. Ask them each to suggest what works well in their partner's flashback scene and if there are any aspects that could be developed further. Display the success criteria.

Assessment opportunity
Children working at levels 4–5 perform their role plays independently. Children working at levels 2–3 work in small groups with a supporting adult. Invite the children to make any changes to their plans to improve them in response to their partner's feedback and then perform the improved role play for the class. Observe children's role plays and make notes. Invite the children watching to comment on the effectiveness of their scenes.

Assessment evidence
Judge the children's self-assessment comments against your own assessment and act on this accordingly. At levels 2–3 children will create a flashback scene that makes sense and contains some appropriate word choices. At levels 4–5 children's flashbacks will be more developed and may include some imaginative detail. Their role plays will include a clear viewpoint. Use children's oral responses during class observation of the role plays and children's improved flashback plans to provide evidence against Writing AF1.

Next steps
Support: Using children's plans/storyboards, help them sequence the events and place the flashback scene at the best moment in the story.
Extension: Invite children to write their flashback scene as a film script.

Key aspects of learning
Enquiry: Children will investigate a film to develop their understanding. They will plan and present their own interpretations of film using different modes of communication.
Creative thinking: Children will generate and extend imaginative ideas, to respond to and interpret ideas. They will suggest hypotheses, responding imaginatively through drama and talk, making connections and understanding relationships to create a written outcome.
Reasoning: Children will draw inferences and make deductions to clarify, extend and follow up ideas and conclusions in their oral and written work.
Evaluation: Children will present information orally, through drama and in writing. They will make judgements and justify their views and opinions, drawing on sources to support their evaluations. Children will discuss success criteria, give feedback to others and judge the effectiveness of their own work.
Communication: Children will develop their skills to reflect critically on what they have seen. They will develop their ability to present a narrative through drama, orally and in writing and reflect critically on their own and others' work.

Periodic assessment

Reading

Learning outcomes
● Children can identify different ways to engage and interrogate text to deepen their understanding.
● Children can identify backgrounds of characters.

Success criteria
● I can compare the usefulness of techniques such as visualisation, prediction and empathy in exploring the meaning of texts.
● I can compare different types of narrative and identify how they are structured.
● I can infer author's perspectives.

Setting the context
This assessment should be carried out once children have completed Narrative Unit 5. Ensure children have experienced analysing the theme, atmosphere and the techniques used by the film maker to achieve these effects in *The Piano* by Aidan Gibbons. Review the work that has been done during the course of this unit and discuss children's achievements with them. Ask them what they found easy to accomplish and what was difficult. Make notes of their responses. Display the success criteria in the classroom. Invite the children to demonstrate their understanding of the work done during the course of the unit by completing the photocopiable page 'Narrative 5 Reading assessment'.

Assessment opportunity
This assessment provides the opportunity to evaluate children's awareness of the progress they have made in understanding how visual narrative structures, such as film, differ from written narratives and to show what they have learned about telling stories through film and the effects of using flashback techniques. For children working at levels 2-3, go through children's responses orally to allow them to clarify their comments.

Assessment evidence
At levels 2-3, children will make comments relating to events recalled from the film. At levels 4-5, children may respond with appropriate references to the film-making techniques such as flashbacks, as well as characterisation and the film makers viewpoint. Use children's oral responses and completed photocopiable pages to provide evidence against Reading AF2 and AF6.

NARRATIVE

Periodic assessment

Writing

Learning outcome
Children can reflect critically on their own writing and edit and improve it.

Success criteria
- I can punctuate sentences accurately using speech marks.
- I can adapt sentence structure to different text-types and readers.

Setting the context
This assessment should be carried out once children have completed Narrative Unit 5. Collect the work that has been completed during the course of Unit 5 and discuss individual children's achievements with them. Ask them to suggest what they found difficult about the writing in the unit and what they found easy to accomplish. Make notes of their responses against the class list. Make a display of children's written outcomes from the unit. Invite children to watch and read each other's work and evaluate their own work against the work of the whole class. Display the success criteria in the classroom. Provide children with the photocopiable page 'Narrative 5 Writing assessment' and invite them to describe two pieces of work they think work well and why, and either another piece of work or aspect of it that could be improved.

Assessment opportunity
This activity provides children with the opportunity to evaluate their own work against the success of the class as a whole and to justify their opinions. It allows children to identify aspects of their work that they think have worked well and also areas where improvements could be made. Invite the children to discuss their own comments written on the photocopiable page and discuss and compare their own opinions with the comments others have made about their own work.

Assessment evidence
Judge the children's self-assessment comments against your own assessment and act on this accordingly. Children's oral responses of their own achievements and their self-evaluations, combined with your own assessments for the work done, can be used to provide evidence against Writing AF1, AF2, AF6 and AF8.

📖SCHOLASTIC

Film order

▪ Cut out and re-order the scenes from *The Piano* to show the sequence of the narrative.

Man playing piano.	Wife sits beside man. They play together.
Wife fades away. Man plays alone.	Man in uniform tries to help dying friend.
Man continues to play the piano alone.	Small boy in old-fashioned brown clothes receives a gift of a hobby horse.
Small boy in modern blue clothes plays with a hobby horse.	Small modern boy and man play together and smile.

Name   Date

Film flashback (1)

🔳 Re-order these pictures to show scenes from a film with a flashback.

🔳 Write a short dialogue for these scenes.

Red
Amber   I can write dialogue for a flashback. 🔲
Green

Illustrations © 2009, Simon Smith / Beehive Illustration.

Name _____   Date _____

Narrative 5 Reading assessment

▪ Fill in the chart to show what you have learned about narrative and film techniques used in *The Piano*.

What I already knew about making films	What I wanted to know	What I did to find out answers	What I learned

I can compare the usefulness of techniques such as visualisation, prediction and empathy in explaining the meaning of texts. ☐

I can compare different types of narrative and identify how they are structured. ☐

I can infer authors' perspectives. ☐

Red ⚪
Amber ⚪
Green ⚪

NARRATIVE
UNIT 6 Dramatic conventions

Literacy objectives

Speak and listen for a wide range of purposes in different contexts
Strand 2 Listening and responding
- Identify some aspects of talk that vary between formal and informal occasions.

Strand 3 Group discussion and interaction
- Plan and manage a group task over time using different levels of planning.
- Understand different ways to take the lead and support others in groups.

Strand 4 Drama
- Perform a scripted scene making use of dramatic conventions.
- Use and recognise the impact of theatrical effects in drama.

Read and write for a range of purposes on paper and on screen
Strand 6 Word structure and spelling
- Spell words containing unstressed vowels.
- Group and classify words according to their spelling patterns and their meanings.

Strand 7 Understanding and interpreting texts
- Compare different types of narrative and information texts and identify how they are structured.
- Explore how writers use language for comic and dramatic effects.

Strand 8 Engaging with and responding to texts
- Compare how a common theme is presented in poetry, prose and other media.

Strand 9 Creating and shaping texts
- Reflect independently and critically on their own writing and edit and improve it.
- Adapt non-narrative forms and styles to write fiction or factual texts, including poems.

Strand 10 Text structure and organisation
- Experiment with the order of sections and paragraphs to achieve different effects.

Strand 11 Sentence structure and punctuation
- Adapt sentence construction to different text-types, purposes and readers.
- Punctuate sentences accurately, including using speech marks and apostrophes.

Strand 12 Presentation
- Use a range of ICT programs to present texts, making informed choices about which electronic tools to use for different purposes.

Key aspects of learning

Enquiry
● Children will ask questions relating to the theme of their scripted presentation, research the relevant content and then plan how to present that content effectively.

Information processing
● Children will identify relevant information from a range of sources on paper and on screen and use this to write their own scripts.

Evaluation
● Children will discuss success criteria, give feedback to others and judge the effectiveness of their own work.

Communication
● Children will develop their ability to analyse and evaluate a range of scripted broadcasts. They will learn how to plan and create a script, including the use of scriptwriting conventions.

Assessment focuses

Reading
AF4 *(identify and comment on the structure and organisation of texts, including grammatical and presentational features at text level).*

Writing
AF2 *(produce texts which are appropriate to task, reader and purpose).*
AF3 *(organise and present whole texts effectively, sequencing and structuring information, ideas and events).*
AF8 *(use correct spelling).*

Speaking and listening
Listening and responding *(give appropriate feedback to peers; ask relevant questions).*
Group discussion and interaction *(actively include and respond to all members of the group; take an active role in a group task over an extended period).*
Drama *(work with others in performance; plan, perform and evaluate performances).*

Resources

Phase 1 activities
Interactive activity, 'Scripts'
Photocopiable page, 'Unstressed vowels'
Interactive activity, 'Unstressed vowels'
Phase 2 activities
Photocopiable page, 'Negative prefixes'
Interactive activity, 'Less common prefixes'
Phase 4 activities
Photocopiable page, 'Broadcast evaluation' (version 1 and 2)
Periodic assessment
Photocopiable page, 'Narrative 6 Writing assessment'

Unit 6 🔲 Dramatic conventions

Learning outcomes	Assessment opportunity and evidence	Assessment focuses (AFs)		Success criteria
		Level 2	Level 3	
Phase ① activities pages 91-92				
Features of scripts Children can recognise the use of a script in a range of broadcast material and can identify the broad purposes of that material.	• Independent activity where children identify features of playscripts and news broadcast scripts and how they differ. • Teacher observation and questioning during the activity and completed interactive activity.	**Reading AF4** Some awareness of use of features of organisation.	**Reading AF4** A few basic features of organisation at text level identified, with little or no linked comment.	• I can compare different types of script and identify how they are structured. • I can use and recognise the impact of theatrical effects in drama.
Unstressed vowels Children can understand the rules for spelling words containing unstressed vowels.	• Independent activity where children identify words with correct spelling and suggest ways to remember them. • Oral feedback and completed interactive activity.	**Writing AF8** • Usually correct spelling of: high frequency grammatical function words; common single morpheme content/lexical words. • Likely errors: inflected endings; phonetic attempts at vowel digraphs.	**Writing AF8** • Correct spelling of: some common grammatical function words; common content/lexical words with more than one morpheme, including compound words. • Likely errors: some inflected endings; some phonetically plausible attempts at content/lexical words.	I can spell words containing unstressed vowels.
Phase ② activity page 93				
Less common prefixes Children know the rules for spelling less common prefixes.	• Independent activity where children choose prefixes to change words from positive to negative forms. • Completed activities on the photocopiable page and children's own oral assessments.	**Writing AF8** • Usually correct spelling of: high frequency grammatical function words; common single morpheme content/lexical words. • Likely errors: inflected endings; phonetic attempts at vowel digraphs.	**Writing AF8** • Correct spelling of: some common grammatical function words; common content/lexical words with more than one morpheme, including compound words. • Likely errors: some inflected endings; some phonetically plausible attempts at content/lexical words.	I know and can use less common prefixes.
Phase ③ activity page 94				
Broadcast news Children can recognise the structure and language features of a range of broadcast material.	• Supported group activity where children write a script for a news broadcast, perform it and evaluate each other's performances. • Teacher observation, children's presentations and written scripts. Peer evaluations.	**Writing AF2** • Some basic purpose established. • Some appropriate features of the given form used. • Some attempts to adopt appropriate style.	**Writing AF2** • Purpose established at a general level. • Main features of selected form sometimes signalled to the reader. • Some attempts at appropriate style, with attention to reader.	• I can use the language and structure of news scripts in my own work. • I can identify some aspects of talk that vary between formal and informal.

Unit 6 Dramatic conventions

Learning outcomes	Assessment opportunity and evidence	Assessment focuses (AFs)		Success criteria
		Level 2	Level 3	
Phase 4 activity page 95				
Evaluating the news • Children can plan, research and write a non-fiction script. • Children can work together to deliver a polished performance of a script and can evaluate their own performance.	• Supported activity where children evaluate their presentations. • Children's scripts, presentations and written evaluations on photocopiable page.	**Writing AF3** • Some basic sequencing of ideas or material. • Openings and/or closings sometimes signalled.	**Writing AF3** • Some attempt to organise ideas with related points placed next to each other. • Openings and closings usually signalled. • Some attempt to sequence ideas or material logically.	I can reflect independently and critically on scripts and presentations.

Learning outcomes	Assessment opportunity and evidence	Assessment focuses (AFs)		Success criteria
		Level 4	Level 5	
Phase 1 activities pages 91–92				
Features of scripts Children can recognise the use of a script in a range of broadcast material and can identify the broad purposes of that material.	• Independent activity where children identify features of playscripts and news broadcast scripts and how they differ. • Oral responses and the completed interactive activity.	**Reading AF4** • Some structural choices identified with simple comment. • Some basic features of organisation at text level identified.	**Reading AF4** • Comments on structural choices show some general awareness of writer's craft. • Various features relating to organisation at text level, including form, are clearly identified, with some explanation.	• I can compare different types of script and identify how they are structured. • I can use and recognise the impact of theatrical effects in drama.
Unstressed vowels Children can understand the rules for spelling words containing unstressed vowels.	• Independent activity where children identify words with correct spelling and suggest ways to remember them. • Oral feedback and completed photocopiable page.	**Writing AF8** • Correct spelling of: most common grammatical function words, including adverbs with -ly formation; regularly formed content/lexical words, including those with multiple morphemes; most past and present tense inflections; plurals. • Likely errors: homophones of some common grammatical function words; occasional phonetically plausible spelling in content/lexical words.	**Writing AF8** • Correct spelling of: grammatical function words; almost all inflected words; most derivational suffixes and prefixes; most content/lexical words. • Likely errors: occasional phonetically plausible spelling of unstressed syllables in content words; double consonants in prefixes.	I can spell words containing unstressed vowels.

Unit 6 ◻ Dramatic conventions

Learning outcomes	Assessment opportunity and evidence	Assessment focuses (AFs)		Success criteria
		Level 4	Level 5	
Phase ② activity page 93				
Less common prefixes Children know the rules for spelling less common prefixes.	• Independent activity where children choose prefixes to change words from positive to negative forms. • Children's completed interactive activity.	**Writing AF8** • Correct spelling of: most common grammatical function words, including adverbs with -ly formation; regularly formed content/ lexical words, including those with multiple morphemes; most past and present tense inflections; plurals. • Likely errors: homophones of some common grammatical function words; occasional phonetically plausible spelling in content/ lexical words.	**Writing AF8** • Correct spelling of: grammatical function words; almost all inflected words; most derivational suffixes and prefixes; most content/ lexical words. • Likely errors: occasional phonetically plausible spelling of unstressed syllables in content words; double consonants in prefixes.	I know and can use less common prefixes.
Phase ③ activity page 94				
Broadcast news Children can recognise the structure and language features of a range of broadcast material.	• Group activity where children write a script for a news broadcast, perform it and evaluate each other's performances. • Teacher observation, children's presentations and written scripts. Peer evaluations.	**Writing AF2** • Main purpose of writing is clear but not always consistently maintained. • Main features of selected form are clear and appropriate to purpose. • Style generally appropriate to task, though awareness of reader not always sustained.	**Writing AF2** • Main purpose of writing is clear and consistently maintained. • Features of selected form clearly established with some adaptation to purpose. • Appropriate style clearly established to maintain reader's interest throughout.	• I can use the language and structure of news scripts in my own work. • I can identify some aspects of talk that vary between formal and informal.
Phase ④ activity page 95				
Evaluating the news • Children can plan, research and write a non-fiction script. • Children can work together to deliver a polished performance of a script and can evaluate their own performance.	• Independent activity where children evaluate their presentations. • Children's scripts, presentations and written evaluations on photocopiable page.	**Writing AF3** • Ideas organised by clustering related points or by time sequence. • Ideas are organised simply with a fitting opening and closing, sometimes linked. • Ideas or material generally in logical sequence but overall direction of writing not always clearly signalled.	**Writing AF3** • Material is structured clearly, with sentences organised into appropriate paragraphs. • Development of material is effectively managed across text. • Overall direction of the text supported by clear links between paragraphs.	I can reflect independently and critically on scripts and presentations.

Phase ① Features of scripts

Learning outcome
Children can recognise the use of a script in a range of broadcast material and can identify the broad purposes of that material.

Success criteria
● I can compare different types of script and identify how they are structured.
● I can use and recognise the impact of theatrical effects in drama.

Setting the context
This assessment should be undertaken once children have explored and compared the language, layout and conventions for scriptwriting in plays and for other broadcasts such as the news. They should have had the opportunity to listen to news broadcasts and discuss reasons why a script is needed. Invite children to do the interactive activity 'Scripts', where they will compare the typical features and conventions of language used in play scriptwriting and news scriptwriting. Ask children, when they have finished, to give you three features that are different about both forms of script.

Assessment opportunity
This assessment provides the opportunity to assess whether children are secure with the conventions and features of playscripts and how they differ from news broadcast scripts, before they look closely at other types of script used in radio and television broadcasting in the next phase of the unit. Observe children working at levels 2–3 and ask them to explain the reasons for their choices of answer on the interactive activity to ensure they are not making guesses.

Assessment evidence
At levels 2–3, children will be able to provide a reason for their answers. At levels 4–5, children will generally answer the questions correctly and will give more detailed explanations of their answers, referring to punctuation, register and tone as well as content. Use children's completed interactive activities and oral responses to provide evidence against Reading AF4.

Next steps
Support: Provide children with short playscripts and news broadcast scripts and encourage them to read them in a role-play situation.
Extension: Invite children to work in a group and to write a script for a 'school news' broadcast.

Key aspects of learning
Communication: Children will develop their ability to analyse and evaluate a range of scripted broadcasts. They will learn how to plan and create a script, including the use of scriptwriting conventions.

NARRATIVE

Phase ① Unstressed vowels

Learning outcome
Children can understand the rules for spelling words containing unstressed vowels.

Success criteria
I can spell words containing unstressed vowels.

Setting the context
This assessment should be undertaken at any point in the unit when children have been revising the spelling of words containing unstressed vowels. Invite children working at levels 2-3 to do the interactive activity 'Unstressed vowels' where they identify the correct spelling of words that are commonly misspelled. For children working at levels 4-5, provide them with the photocopiable page 'Unstressed vowels'. When children have finished, ask them to think up ways of remembering how to spell words with unstressed vowels. Invite them to share these ideas with the class. Compare their ideas and choose the best ones.

Assessment opportunity
This assessment activity provides the opportunity to assess whether children are secure with the spelling patterns of words containing unstressed vowels and their ability to recognise wrongly spelled words out of context.

Assessment evidence
At levels 2-3 children may need to use a dictionary or take two attempts to get all the answers correct. At levels 4-5, children will mostly identify the missing vowels without needing to refer to a dictionary. Use children's completed activity and oral responses to provide evidence against Writing AF8.

Next steps
Support: Provide children with three words containing unstressed vowels to take home and practise spelling. These can be words they spelled incorrectly in the assessment activity.
Extension: Invite children to invent memory-joggers or mnemonics for tricky words with unstressed vowels.

Key aspects of learning
Evaluation: Children will discuss success criteria, give feedback to others and judge the effectiveness of their own work.

Phase ② Less common prefixes

NARRATIVE

Learning outcome
Children know the rules for spelling less common prefixes.

Success criteria
I know and can use less common prefixes.

Setting the context
This assessment activity should be undertaken as part of children's work on scripts and scriptwriting when you have revised the use of less common prefixes during shared and guided reading and writing. For children working at level 3 or lower, provide copies of the photocopiable page 'Negative prefixes' and ask them to change the underlined words to negative forms by adding a prefix. Ask children working at levels 4–5 to complete the interactive activity 'Less common prefixes'.

Assessment opportunity
Ask children working at levels 2–3 to read the sentences aloud using the negative words. Ask them if they sound right and get them to change any that do not. Ask them if there are any prefixes they find difficult to use. Use their oral responses and completed photocopiable pages to demonstrate their confidence in using less familiar prefixes. Make notes of their oral responses. Children working at levels 4–5 can complete the interactive activity independently.

Assessment evidence
At levels 2–3 children may confuse the prefixes 'ir', 'il' and 'im', using 'un' in error, for example, they might write 'unreplaceable' rather than 'irreplaceable'. At levels 4–5 children will score highly in the interactive activity. Use children's oral responses and completed activities to provide evidence against Writing AF8.

Next steps
Support: Revise other negative prefixes during guided reading when the opportunity arises during the course of the unit.
Extension: Invite children to collect words with unusual or less common prefixes in their reading journals from independent reading.

Key aspects of learning
Evaluation: Children will discuss success criteria, give feedback to others and judge the effectiveness of their own work.

NARRATIVE

Phase ③ Broadcast news

Learning outcome
Children can recognise the structure and language features of a range of broadcast material.

Success criteria
- I can use the language and structure of news scripts in my own work.
- I can identify some aspects of talk that vary between formal and informal.

Setting the context
This assessment should be undertaken after the children have explored and analysed the features and conventions of writing news broadcast scripts in shared and guided writing. Together create a brief list of newsworthy stories about the class or school and write them on the board. Ask children to work in groups of three and choose three stories from the list. Ask them to write one of their three chosen stories each as a script for a news broadcast. Tell them then to make a choice of the most suitable running order, and the roles they should take to perform their news broadcasts. Children working at levels 2–3 should work with a supporting adult.

Assessment opportunity
This assessment provides the opportunity to evaluate how well children have understood the features and use of language in writing a script for a news broadcast and their ability to collaborate to make decisions as a group. Invite groups of children to perform their news broadcast for the class. Observe children's role plays and make notes. Invite the children watching to comment on the effectiveness of the scripts and role play. Ask them to suggest two things that worked well in the script and one aspect that could be improved. Make notes on their responses.

Assessment evidence
At levels 2-3 children will create a short report on each story, in a logical running order. They may use informal language rather than formal. Children working at levels 4-5 will create more detailed reports using standard English. They will link more confidently between anchor and on-site reporters. Use children's oral responses during class observation of the role plays and children's written scripts to provide evidence against Writing AF2.

Next steps
Support: Invite children to listen and watch radio and television newscasts to collect sentences and phrases to link their own news stories.
Extension: Invite children to collect suitable school stories and events over the course of a week to write and perform an end-of-week news bulletin.

Key aspects of learning
Enquiry: Children will ask questions relating to the theme of their scripted presentation, research the relevant content and then plan how to present that content effectively.
Information processing: Children will identify relevant information from a range of sources on paper and on screen and use this to write their own scripts.
Evaluation: Children will discuss success criteria, give feedback to others and judge the effectiveness of their own work.
Communication: Children will develop their ability to analyse and evaluate a range of scripted broadcasts. They will learn how to plan and create a script, including the use of scriptwriting conventions.

Phase ④ Evaluating the news

Learning outcomes

● Children can plan, research and write a non-fiction script.
● Children can work together to deliver a polished performance of a script and can evaluate their own performance.

Success criteria

I can reflect independently and critically on scripts and presentations.

Setting the context

This assessment should be undertaken after the children have analysed the conventions of writing news broadcast scripts in shared and guided writing. They should have worked in groups to create a news broadcast, first gathering content, then scriptwriting, polishing and producing their presentation using digital video recorders and video software. Display the success criteria in the classroom. Explain that they are going to evaluate their own group's presentations using certain criteria on the photocopiable page 'Broadcast evaluation' (versions 1 or 2). Children working at levels 4–5 can evaluate their group's performance independently. Children working at levels 2–3 should work with a supporting adult to discuss their responses to the questions on version 1 of the photocopiable page.

Assessment opportunity

This assessment provides the opportunity to evaluate how well children have understood the features and use of language in writing a script for a news broadcast, how well they put the conventions into practice and their ability to evaluate the whole group's joint performance.

Assessment evidence

Make judgements about children's assessments of their group's presentation against your own assessments. Use children's evaluations together with their video presentations and written scripts to provide evidence against Writing AF3.

Next steps

Support: Invite children to share their group's individual responses and discuss how to improve their presentations.
Extension: Invite children to present their news broadcasts using their written scripts to a wider audience, for example another class or school assembly.

Key aspects of learning

Enquiry: Children ask questions relating to the theme of their scripted presentation, research the relevant content and then plan how to present that content effectively.
Information processing: Children will identify relevant information from a range of sources on paper and on screen and use this to write their own scripts.
Evaluation: Children will discuss success criteria, give feedback to others and judge the effectiveness of their own work.
Communication: Children will develop their ability to evaluate a range of scripted broadcasts. They will learn how to create a script, using scriptwriting conventions.

NARRATIVE

Periodic assessment

Reading

Learning outcomes
• Children can identify differences between written playscripts and news scripts.
• Children can identify language features of news.

Success criteria
• I can compare different types of script and explain how they are structured.
• I can explain how aspects of talk vary in formal and informal situations.

Setting the context
This assessment should be carried out once the children have completed Narrative Unit 6. Ensure they have analysed the conventions and structures of different types of script, including plays, films and non-fiction scripts. Review the work that has been done during the course of the unit and discuss children's achievements with them. Make notes of their responses.

Assessment opportunity
Invite individual children to describe orally how a playscript is different from a news broadcast script in layout and language. Make notes of their responses. For children working at levels 2–3, ask questions to draw out their responses such as: *Is a news script fiction or non-fiction? How would you write the names of the people involved in a news broadcast compared with the way you write the cast for a play? How does a playscript signal the end of a section? How does a news script signal a change in the news item?*

Assessment evidence
At levels 2–3, children demonstrate a need for prompting to recall the differences in the types of script. At levels 4–5, children can explain how they differ independently. Use children's oral responses and evidence collected over the course of the unit to provide evidence against Reading AF4 and AF5.

Writing

Learning outcome
Children can evaluate their own work in writing and analysing different types of script.

Success criteria
I can reflect independently and critically on my own writing.

Setting the context
Display the children's written work from the unit. Invite the children to read each other's work and evaluate it against the work of the whole class. Provide children with the photocopiable page 'Narrative 6 Writing assessment'. invite them to describe two pieces of work they think work well, and an aspect that could be improved.

Assessment opportunity
This activity provides the children with an opportunity to evaluate their own work against the success of the whole class. Invite the children to discuss their own comments written on the photocopiable page and compare their own opinions with the comments others have made about their own work.

Assessment evidence
Judge the children's self-assessment comments against your own assessment and act on this accordingly. Provide the children with constructive comments and manageable targets for future writing. Children's oral responses and their self-evaluations can be used to provide evidence against Writing AF2.

NARRATIVE

Name   Date

Unstressed vowels

■ Look at the words in the column on the left. The unstressed vowels have been left out of these words. Use a dictionary to help you find the missing vowels, write the missing vowel in the next column and then rewrite the words correctly. The first has been done as an example.

Incorrect spelling	Missing vowel	Correct spelling
necessry	*a*	*necessary*
histry		
memrable		
frightning		
confrence		
desprate		
compny		
refrence		
litrature		
revolutionry		

Red
Amber   I can spell words containing unstressed vowels. ☐
Green

NON-FICTION
Unit 1 Instructions

Literacy objectives

Speak and listen for a wide range of purposes in different contexts
Strand 2 Listening and responding
● Identify some aspects of talk that vary between formal and informal occasions.

Read and write for a range of purposes on paper and on screen
Strand 7 Understanding and interpreting texts
● Compare different types of narrative and information texts and identify how they are structured.
Strand 8 Engaging with and responding to texts
● Compare the usefulness of techniques such as visualisation, prediction and empathy in exploring the meaning of texts.
Strand 9 Creating and shaping texts
● Reflect independently and critically on their own writing and edit and improve it.
● Adapt non-narrative forms and styles to write fiction or factual texts, including poems.
● Vary the pace and develop the viewpoint through the use of direct and reported speech, portrayal of action and selection of detail.
● Create multi-layered texts, including use of hyperlinks and linked web pages.
Strand 10 Text structure and organisation
● Experiment with the order of sections and paragraphs to achieve different effects.
● Change the order of material within a paragraph, moving the topic sentence.
Strand 11 Sentence structure and punctuation
● Adapt sentence construction to different text-types, purposes and readers.
● Punctuate sentences accurately, including using speech marks and apostrophes.
Strand 12 Presentation
● Use a range of ICT programs to present texts, making informed choices about which electronic tools to use for different purposes.

Key aspects of learning

Enquiry
● Children will investigate a range of instructional texts by asking relevant questions, researching and following instructions to explore their effectiveness.
Information processing
● Children will identify relevant information from a range of sources on paper and on screen and use this as a basis for both oral and written instructions.
Evaluation
● Children will read, compare and evaluate instructional texts from a variety of sources. When presenting instructional texts orally and in writing, they will discuss success criteria, give feedback to others and judge the effectiveness of their own work.
Reasoning
● Children will draw on their understanding and use of instructional texts to construct reasoned opinions and arguments based on available information and evidence.

Key aspects of learning (contd)

Empathy
- In discussing and writing about real or simulated events, children will need to imagine themselves in another person's position.

Communication
- Children will develop their skills to reflect critically on what they have seen and read. They will develop their ability to give and follow clear instructions and reflect on the effectiveness of different modes of communication. They will work collaboratively in pairs and groups, and outcomes will be both oral and written.

Assessment focuses

Reading
AF4 *(identify and comment on the structure and organisation of texts, including grammatical and presentational features at text level).*
AF5 *(explain and comment on writers' use of language, including grammatical and literary features at word and sentence level).*

Writing
AF2 *(produce texts which are appropriate to task, reader and purpose).*
AF3 *(organise and present whole texts effectively, sequencing and structuring information, ideas and events).*

Speaking and listening
Listening and responding (listen to and understand main points of instruction text; respond appropriately).

Resources

Phase 1 activities
Photocopiable page, 'Sequencing instructions' (versions 1 and 2)
Photocopiable page, 'Treasure map'
Phase 2 activities
Photocopiable page, 'How to make a thaumatrope' (a)
Photocopiable page, 'How to make a thaumatrope' (b)
Interactive activity, 'How to make a thaumatrope'
Phase 3 activities
Photocopiable page, 'Writing for a younger reader (versions 1 and 2)'
Periodic assessment
Photocopiable page, 'Non-fiction 1 Reading assessment'
Interactive activity, 'Non-fiction 1 Reading assessment'

Unit 1 ⬜ Instructions

Learning outcomes	Assessment opportunity and evidence	Assessment focuses (AFs)		Success criteria
		Level 2	Level 3	
Phase ① activities pages 103–104				
Sequencing instructions ● Children demonstrate that they can use more formal aspects of language in a role play situation. ● Children can identify some of the difficulties that may arise if one or more communication modes are not available.	● Paired activity where children discuss and then sequence a set of instructions. ● Children's oral responses, notes made against the class list and completed interactive activity or photocopiable page.	**Reading AF4** ● Some awareness of use of features of organisation. **Reading AF5** ● Some effective language choices noted. ● Some familiar patterns of language identified.	**Reading AF4** ● A few basic features of organisation at text level identified, with little or no linked comment. **Reading AF5** ● A few basic features of writer's use of language identified, but with little or no comment.	● I can understand the difference between talk which may vary between formal and informal. ● I can compare the usefulness of techniques in giving instructions.
Finding the treasure ● Children can identify some of the difficulties that may arise if one or more communication modes are not available. ● Children understand the need for courtesy, patience and a shared technical vocabulary.	● Paired activity where one child gives the other route instructions to follow and they then check the completed routes for accuracy. ● Children's self- and paired assessments.	**Writing AF3** ● Some basic sequencing of ideas or material. ● Openings and/or closings sometimes signalled.	**Writing AF3** ● Some attempt to organise ideas with related points placed next to each other. ● Openings and closings usually signalled. ● Some attempt to sequence ideas or material logically.	● I can understand the difference between talk which may vary between formal and informal. ● I can compare the usefulness of techniques in giving instructions. ● I can understand the need for courtesy and patience.
Phase ② activities pages 105–106				
How to make a thaumatrope ● Children can identify and understand key features and conventions of instructional texts. ● Children demonstrate that they can evaluate sets of instructions (including attempting to follow some of them) for purpose, organisation and layout, clarity and usefulness.	● Paired activity where children compare, follow and evaluate two different sets of instructions. ● Children's oral feedback and written responses on the photocopiable page.	**Reading AF4** ● Some awareness of use of features of organisation.	**Reading AF4** ● A few basic features of organisation at text level identified, with little or no linked comment.	I can compare different types of instruction text and identify how they are structured.
Clear instructions Children demonstrate that they can evaluate sets of instructions (including attempting to follow some of them) for purpose, organisation and layout, clarity and usefulness.	● Paired activity where children follow each other's instructions, evaluate them and then edit and improve their writing. ● Children's oral comments, self-assessments and written instructions.	**Writing AF2** ● Some basic purpose established. ● Some appropriate features of the given form used. ● Some attempts to adopt appropriate style.	**Writing AF2** ● Purpose established at a general level. ● Main features of selected form sometimes signalled to the reader. ● Some attempts at appropriate style, with attention to reader.	I can evaluate my own written instructions for clarity and organisation.

Unit 1 ▢ Instructions

Learning outcomes	Assessment opportunity and evidence	Assessment focuses (AFs)		Success criteria
		Level 2	Level 3	
Phase ③ activity page 107				
Writing for a younger reader • Children demonstrate that they can write an instructional text using appropriate form and features and awareness of intended audience. • Children can reflect on their writing and edit and improve it, showing a clear understanding of the features of instructional writing.	• Supported group activity where children rewrite instructional text for a younger audience using a flow chart writing frame. • Children's written outcomes on photocopiable page and notes against the class list.	**Writing AF2** • Some basic purpose established. • Some appropriate features of the given form used. • Some attempts to adopt appropriate style.	**Writing AF2** • Purpose established at a general level. • Main features of selected form sometimes signalled to the reader. • Some attempts at appropriate style, with attention to reader.	• I can write an instructional text and adapt sentence construction to different purposes and readers. • I can reflect critically on my own writing and edit and improve it.

Learning outcomes	Assessment opportunity and evidence	Assessment focuses (AFs)		Success criteria
		Level 4	Level 5	
Phase ① activities pages 103-104				
Sequencing instructions • Children demonstrate that they can use more formal aspects of language in a role play situation. • Children can identify some of the difficulties that may arise if one or more communication modes are not available.	• Independent activity where children discuss and then sequence a set of instructions. • Children's oral responses, notes made against the class list and completed interactive activity or photocopiable page.	**Reading AF4** • Some structural choices identified with simple comment. • Some basic features of organisation at text level identified. **Reading AF5** • Some basic features of writer's use of language identified. • Simple comments on writer's choices.	**Reading AF4** • Comments on structural choices show some general awareness of author's craft. • Various features relating to organisation at text level, including form, are clearly identified, with some explanation. **Reading AF5** • Various features of writer's use of language identified, with some explanation. • Comments show some awareness of the effect of writer's language choices.	• I can understand the difference between talk which may vary between formal and informal. • I can compare the usefulness of techniques in giving instructions.
Finding the treasure • Children can identify some of the difficulties that may arise if one or more communication modes are not available. • Children understand the need for courtesy, patience and a shared technical vocabulary.	• Paired activity where one child gives the other route instructions to follow and they then check the completed routes for accuracy. • Children's self- and paired assessments.	**Writing AF3** • Ideas organised by clustering related points or by time sequence. • Ideas are organised simply with a fitting opening and closing, sometimes linked. • Ideas or material generally in logical sequence but overall direction of writing not always clearly signalled.	**Writing AF3** • Material is structured clearly, with sentences organised into appropriate paragraphs. • Development of material is effectively managed across text. • Overall direction of the text supported by clear links between paragraphs.	• I can understand the difference between talk which may vary between formal and informal. • I can compare the usefulness of techniques in giving instructions. • I can understand the need for courtesy and patience.

Unit 1 ◻ Instructions

Learning outcomes	Assessment opportunity and evidence	Assessment focuses (AFs)		Success criteria
		Level 4	Level 5	
Phase ② activities pages 105–106				
How to make a thaumatrope • Children can identify and understand key features and conventions of instructional texts. • Children demonstrate that they can evaluate sets of instructions (including attempting to follow some of them) for purpose, organisation and layout, clarity and usefulness.	• Paired activity where children compare, follow and evaluate two different sets of instructions. • Children's oral feedback and written responses on the photocopiable page.	**Reading AF4** • Some structural choices identified with simple comment. • Some basic features of organisation at text level identified.	**Reading AF4** • Comments on structural choices show some general awareness of writer's craft. • Various features relating to organisation at text level, including form, are clearly identified, with some explanation.	I can compare different types of instruction text and identify how they are structured.
Clear instructions Children demonstrate that they can evaluate sets of instructions (including attempting to follow some of them) for purpose, organisation and layout, clarity and usefulness.	• Paired activity where children follow each other's instructions, evaluate them and then edit and improve their writing. • Children's oral comments, self-assessments and written instructions.	**Writing AF2** • Main purpose of writing is clear but not always consistently maintained. • Main features of selected form are clear and appropriate to purpose. • Style generally appropriate to task, though awareness of reader not always sustained.	**Writing AF2** • Main purpose of writing is clear and consistently maintained. • Features of selected form clearly established with some adaptation to purpose. • Appropriate style clearly established to maintain reader's interest throughout.	I can evaluate my own written instructions for clarity and organisation.
Phase ③ activity page 107				
Writing for a younger reader • Children demonstrate that they can write an instructional text using appropriate form and features and awareness of intended audience. • Children can reflect on their writing and edit and improve it, showing a clear understanding of the features of instructional writing.	• Independent activity where children rewrite instructional text for a younger audience using a flow chart writing frame. • Children's written outcomes on photocopiable page.	**Writing AF2** • Main purpose of writing is clear but not always consistently maintained. • Main features of selected form are clear and appropriate to purpose. • Style generally appropriate to task, though awareness of reader not always sustained.	**Writing AF2** • Main purpose of writing is clear and consistently maintained. • Features of selected form clearly established with some adaptation to purpose. • Appropriate style clearly established to maintain reader's interest throughout.	• I can write an instructional text and adapt sentence construction to different purposes and readers. • I can reflect critically on my own writing and edit and improve it.

Phase ① Sequencing instructions

Learning outcomes
- Children can demonstrate that they use more formal aspects of language in a role-play situation.
- Children can identify some of the difficulties that may arise if one or more communication modes are not available.

Success criteria
- I can understand the difference between talk which may vary between formal and informal.
- I can compare the usefulness of techniques in giving instructions.

Setting the context
This assessment should be carried out once children have had the opportunity to explore the language of instructions through playing barrier games in pairs, with one giving oral instructions to the other. Discuss the type of language used. Ask them to describe how well they conveyed information to a listener and how easily they were able to follow each other's instructions. Ask them how they were able to make their instructions clear. What positional language did they need to use? Did they vary their sentences? Did they use any time-related connectives? Invite children to sequence a set of instructions using the photocopiable page 'Sequencing instructions' (version 1 or 2). Ask children working at levels 2-3 to use version 1 of the photocopiable page.

Assessment opportunity
Children working at levels 2-3 should work with a partner to read and discuss the instructions before collaborating to put them into the correct sequence. When children have sequenced their instructions, invite them to use a computer to carry out the instructions. One partner, without seeing the computer screen being used, reads the instructions while the other follows the instructions to create a multiple-choice quiz using PowerPoint® software. Invite children to say how easy or difficult it was to follow the instructions. Ask them to suggest what they could add to make them easier or clearer to follow. Make notes of their responses. Children working at levels 4-5 can work independently to sequence the instructions, using version 2 of photocopiable page, but they will need a partner for the second part of the activity.

Assessment evidence
At levels 2-3, children may use the time-based connectives 'first' and 'finally' to begin and end the sequence, but may make mistakes about the order of others. Use your notes, oral responses and completed interactive activity or photocopiable page to provide evidence against Reading AF4 and AF5.

Next steps
Support: Provide children with a clear list of tips for writing good instructions.
Extension: Invite children to write a clearer step-by-step set of instructions for creating an interactive multiple-choice quiz.

Key aspects of learning
Enquiry: Children will investigate a range of instructional texts by asking relevant questions, researching and following instructions to explore their effectiveness.
Information processing: Children will identify relevant information from a range of sources on paper and on screen and use this as a basis for both oral and written instructions.
Evaluation: Children will read, compare and evaluate instructional texts from a variety of sources. When presenting instructional texts orally and in writing, they will discuss success criteria, give feedback to others and judge the effectiveness of their own work.
Communication: Children will develop their skills to reflect critically on what they have seen and read. They will develop their ability to give and follow clear instructions and reflect on the effectiveness of different modes of communication. They will work collaboratively in pairs and groups, and outcomes will be both oral and written.

Phase ① Finding the treasure

Learning outcomes
- Children can identify some of the difficulties that may arise if one or more communication modes are not available.
- Children understand the need for courtesy, patience and a shared technical vocabulary.

Success criteria
- I can understand the difference between talk which may vary between formal and informal.
- I can compare the usefulness of techniques in giving instructions.
- I can understand the need for courtesy and patience.

Setting the context
This assessment activity should be undertaken once children have had opportunities to give others oral instructions to go somewhere or find something with a partner, with one giving the instructions and the other following them while blindfolded. They should also have explored the use of punctuation in instructions, particularly the use of commas to separate dependent clauses and parenthetic commas to separate phrases. Enlarge and display the map on the photocopiable page 'Treasure map'. Discuss how someone would get from A to B and how to communicate this to someone who was blindfolded. Ask children to work with a partner. Provide one of the pair with a copy of the photocopiable page and their partner with a sheet of tracing paper. Give both children a coloured marker and a ruler. Sitting back to back, invite one pupil to draw each step from A to B and describe it to their partner, using a marker and a ruler to give accurate detailed instructions. The pupil using tracing paper marks each step on the paper. When they have finished, place the paper over the map and they compare the marked route. Ask them to evaluate their oral instructions. Have they been able to draw the same route? Were the instructions clear and detailed? Did they have the patience to describe the route slowly and carefully, and repeat instructions where necessary?

Assessment opportunity
This activity provides an opportunity for children to evaluate their own and a partner's ability to give detailed oral instructions. Observe pairs of children as they instruct their partner and make notes against the class list.

Assessment evidence
Use children's self- and paired assessments judged against your own observations to provide evidence against Writing AF3.

Next steps
Support: For children who struggled to give clearly detailed instructions, provide them with instructions to study with outcomes that depend on accuracy, for example, driving directions, recipes.
Extension: Invite children to write their own 'treasure island' instructions.

Key aspects of learning
Evaluation: Children will read, compare and evaluate instructional texts from a variety of sources. When presenting instructional texts orally and in writing, they will discuss success criteria, give feedback to others and judge the effectiveness of their own work.
Reasoning: Children will draw on their understanding and use of instructional texts to construct reasoned opinions and arguments based on available information and evidence.
Communication: Children will develop their skills to reflect critically on what they have seen and read. They will develop their ability to give and follow clear instructions and reflect on the effectiveness of different modes of communication. They will work collaboratively in pairs and groups, and outcomes will be both oral and written.

Phase ② How to make a thaumatrope

Learning outcomes

- Children can identify and understand key features and conventions of instructional texts.
- Children demonstrate that they can evaluate sets of instructions (including attempting to follow some of them) for purpose, organisation and layout, clarity and usefulness.

Success criteria

I can compare different types of instruction text and identify how they are structured.

Setting the context

This assessment should be carried out after the children have had practice at giving and following oral sets of instructions. They should have explored the typical language, layout and features of different sets of instructions in shared and guided reading. Provide the children with the photocopiable pages 'How to make a thaumatrope' (a) and (b). Ask them to compare both sets of instructions with a partner. Provide them with the necessary equipment and invite one pupil to follow the photocopiable (a) instructions and the other to follow the instructions on photocopiable (b). When they finish, ask them to annotate the layout and language features of their instructions and evaluate them at the bottom of the page.

Assessment opportunity

This activity provides the opportunity to evaluate children's understanding of the layout and language in sets of instructions. Provide a list of key features for children working at levels 2-3 to support them when annotating their page. Observe children as they follow the instructions. When they have evaluated their own set of instructions, ask pairs of children to say which set were clearer or easier to follow and why.

Assessment evidence

Children may suggest that the instructions on photocopiable page 'How to make a thaumatrope (a)' were clearer based on the layout. However children should have identified the photocopiable page 'How to make a thaumatrope (b)' instructions as being more precise and easy to follow. Use children's oral and written evaluations to provide evidence against Reading AF4.

Next steps

Support: Children who demonstrate insecurity about language and layout of instructions can complete the interactive activity 'How to make a thaumatrope'.
Extension: Invite children to improve the instructions on their photocopiable page.

Key aspects of learning

Enquiry: Children will investigate a range of instructional texts by asking relevant questions, researching and following instructions to explore their effectiveness.
Evaluation: Children will read, compare and evaluate instructional texts from a variety of sources. When presenting instructional texts orally and in writing, they will discuss success criteria, give feedback to others and judge the effectiveness of their own work.
Reasoning: Children will draw on their understanding and use of instructional texts to construct reasoned opinions and arguments based on available information and evidence.
Communication: Children will develop their skills to reflect critically on what they have seen and read. They will develop their ability to give and follow clear instructions and reflect on the effectiveness of different modes of communication. They will work collaboratively in pairs and groups, and outcomes will be both oral and written.

Phase ② Clear instructions

Learning outcome

Children demonstrate that they can evaluate sets of instructions (including attempting to follow some of them) for purpose, organisation and layout, clarity and usefulness.

Success criteria

I can evaluate my own written instructions for clarity and organisation.

Setting the context

This assessment should be undertaken after the children have written their own sets of instructions during shared, guided and independent writing sessions. They should have written a set of instructions to tell someone how to create an image or file on a computer. Ask the children to work in pairs and take turns to put each other's instructions into practice, one reading the instructions and the other following them. Encourage the one following the instructions to ask questions to clarify the instructions when they are at all unclear about what to do. Ask the children to edit and improve their own instructions based on the clarification needed by their partner.

Assessment opportunity

This activity provides an opportunity for children to assess the clarity and usefulness of their own written instructions. Support children working at level 3 or lower by suggesting question types to use before they begin, for example: *Do I double click on the icon or single click? Where do I find it on the screen? How big should I make the shape?* Ask the children for feedback about what was needed to clarify their own instructions.

Assessment evidence

Children working at levels 2-3 may not always ask appropriate questions that clarify unclear instructions. Make notes against the class list of children's oral responses and use the edited and improved sets of instructions to provide evidence against Writing AF2.

Next steps

Support: Make a class collection of instructions where clarity is particularly vital, for example, on health and safety issues, taking prescription medicines and so on, for reference.

Extension: Encourage children to look out for badly written instructions and to rewrite them, for example, how to assemble furniture, set up a DVD player and so on.

Key aspects of learning

Evaluation: Children will read, compare and evaluate instructional texts from a variety of sources. When presenting instructional texts orally and in writing, they will discuss success criteria, give feedback to others and judge the effectiveness of their own work.

Reasoning: Children will draw on their understanding and use of instructional texts to construct reasoned opinions and arguments based on available information and evidence.

Empathy: In discussing and writing about real or simulated events, children will need to imagine themselves in another person's position.

Communication: Children will develop their skills to reflect critically on what they have seen and read. They will develop their ability to give and follow clear instructions and reflect on the effectiveness of different modes of communication. They will work collaboratively in pairs and groups, and outcomes will be both oral and written.

Phase ③ Writing for a younger reader

Learning outcomes

- Children demonstrate that they can write an instructional text using appropriate form and features and awareness of intended audience.
- Children can reflect on their writing and edit and improve it, showing a clear understanding of the features of instructional writing.

Success criteria

- I can write an instructional text and adapt sentence construction to different purposes and readers.
- I can reflect critically on my own writing and edit and improve it.

Setting the context

This assessment should be undertaken after the children have had experience of exploring instructional texts through shared, guided and independent reading and writing. They should have had practice at drafting, writing and improving instructional texts written for a variety of purposes and for different audiences. Explain to the children that they are going to revisit a set of instructions written during the course of the unit and edit them so that they are suitable for much younger children to follow. Provide the children with copies of the photocopiable page 'Writing for a younger reader' (version 1 or 2) and ask them to make notes on the frame to revise their instructions for younger readers. Children working at levels 2-3 work in a group with a supporting adult and use the flow chart frame on version 1. Children working at levels 4-5 work independently using version 2.

Assessment opportunity

Use this activity as an opportunity to evaluate children's awareness of how the intended audience affects the use of language and to assess their ability to precis their texts while retaining essential information. An adult working with the supported group can ask questions to help children choose appropriate vocabulary and sentence structures, and make notes against the class list.

Assessment evidence

Children working at levels 4-5 demonstrate more awareness of the need to adjust the language of their instructions for a different audience than those at levels 2-3. Use children's completed photocopiable pages to provide evidence against Writing AF2.

Next steps

Support: Children work in a supported group to write a polished set of instructions.
Extension: Children independently write a polished set of instructions.

Key aspects of learning

Enquiry: Children will investigate a range of instructional texts by asking relevant questions, researching and following instructions to explore their effectiveness.
Evaluation: Children will read, compare and evaluate instructional texts from a variety of sources. When presenting instructional texts orally and in writing, they will discuss success criteria, give feedback to others and judge the effectiveness of their own work.
Reasoning: Children will draw on their understanding and use of instructional texts to construct reasoned opinions and arguments based on available information and evidence.
Empathy: In discussing and writing about real or simulated events, children will need to imagine themselves in another person's position.
Communication: Children will develop their skills to reflect critically on what they have seen and read. They will develop their ability to give and follow clear instructions and reflect on the effectiveness of different modes of communication. They will work collaboratively in pairs and groups, and outcomes will be both oral and written.

Periodic assessment

Reading

Learning outcome
Children demonstrate that they can evaluate sets of instructions (including attempting to follow some of them) for purpose, organisation and layout, clarity and usefulness.

Success criteria
I can identify the language, features and structure of instruction texts.

Setting the context
This assessment should be carried out once children have completed Non-fiction Unit 1. Ensure children have had experience of reading, comparing and analysing a variety of different instructional texts during shared, guided and independent reading. Review the work that has been done during the course of this unit and discuss children's achievements with them. Ask them what they found easy to accomplish and what was difficult. Make notes of their responses against the class list. Invite children working at levels 4-5 to do the interactive 'Non-fiction 1 Reading assessment' activity as a group. Children select 'always', 'never' or 'sometimes' in response to statements about instructional text. Encourage children to justify their answers by giving examples, particularly when they select 'sometimes' as their answer. Children working at level 3 or lower do the activity using the photocopiable page 'Non-fiction 1 Reading assessment' in a supported group. They cut out the statements and group them into piles according to 'always', 'never' or 'sometimes' and give reasons for their choices to the supporting adult.

Assessment opportunity
Use the interactive activity and the photocopiable page activity to assess children's confidence in their knowledge of the typical language and layout features of instructions. Make notes of individual children's responses.

Assessment evidence
Children working at levels 2–3 show they are not completely secure in selecting answers for the 'sometimes' category. Children working at levels 4-5 are mostly confident in their knowledge of the features. Use children's interactive responses, supported group activity and oral responses to provide judgements against Reading AF4 and AF5.

Periodic assessment

Writing

Learning outcomes
- Children demonstrate that they can write an instructional text using appropriate form and features and awareness of intended audience.
- Children can reflect on their writing and edit and improve it, showing a clear understanding of the features of instructional writing.

Success criteria
- I can use appropriate sentence construction, form and features when writing an instructional text.
- I can reflect independently and critically on my own writing and edit and improve it.

Setting the context
This assessment should be carried out once children have completed Non-fiction Unit 1 'Instructions'. Collect the work that has been completed during the course of Unit 1 and discuss individual children's achievements with them. Ask them to suggest what they found difficult about the work in the unit and what they found easy to accomplish. Make notes of their responses against the class list. Ask children to choose a piece of instruction writing done at the beginning of the unit. Ask them to swap with a partner. Tell them to read their partner's work and describe what they think is needed to polish it. Invite them to revise their own writing, taking account of what they have learnt during the whole unit and their partner's comments.

Assessment opportunity
When children have added to or revised their instructions, they swap them with their partners again. Invite the partners to evaluate what they have done to improve and polish the instructions. This activity provides an opportunity to assess children's abilities to evaluate their own or another's writing.

Assessment evidence
Children's oral responses of their own achievements, their partner's evaluations of their completed instructions and own observations during the course of the unit can be used to provide evidence against Writing AF3.

Treasure map

Illustration © 2009, Simon Smith/Beehive Illustration.

Name   Date

NON-FICTION

How to make a thaumatrope (a)

What you need:

2 cardboard circles

a hole punch

crayons

2 pieces of string

What you do:

1. Draw a bird cage on one circle and colour it black.

2. Draw a bird on the other circle and colour it blue.

3. Punch a hole at either side of each card circle.

4. Place the cards together.

5. Thread and tie a piece of string through each hole.

6. Twist the string tightly.

7. Gently pull the string to untwist it and spin the thaumatrope.

8. What can you see?

How easy was it to follow these instructions and why?

_____

_____

_____

What is needed to improve these instructions?

_____

_____

_____

_____

Red
Amber
Green

I can compare different types of instruction text and identify how they are structured. ☐

Illustration © 2009, Simon Smith/Beehive Illustration.

NON-FICTION

Name   Date

Writing for a younger reader (1)

How to:

What you need:

What you do:

1.

2.

3.

4.

I can write an instructional text and adapt sentence construction to different purposes and readers. ☐

I can reflect critically on my own writing and edit and improve it. ☐

Red
Amber
Green

Non-fiction 1 Reading assessment

◀ Cut out the statements and group them into piles of 'sometimes', 'always' or 'never'.

Instructions tell the reader how to do or make something.

Instructions use bullet points.

Instructions need diagrams.

Instructions use imperative verbs.

A verb is used to begin each sentence in instructions.

Instructions can be read in any order.

Instructions are linked by connectives.

Instructions are written in a numbered list.

Time-based connectives are used in a list of instructions.

Instructions are written in the past tense.

Instructions explain why or how something happens.

The list of materials needed is written in the order they will be used.

Instructions include advice or warnings.

The title of a set of instructions tells you the intended outcome.

Instructions can use persuasive language.

Instructions use precise language.

Instructions describe something that happened in the past.

Instructions use passive verbs.

NON-FICTION

UNIT 2 Recounts

Literacy objectives

Speak and listen for a wide range of purposes in different contexts

Strand 1 Speaking
- Use and explore different question types and different ways words are used, including in formal and informal contexts.

Strand 2 Listening and responding
- Identify different question types and evaluate their impact on the audience.
- Identify some aspects of talk that vary between formal and informal occasions.

Strand 3 Group discussion and interaction
- Plan and manage a group task over time using different levels of planning.
- Understand different ways to take the lead and support others in groups.
- Understand the process of decision making.

Strand 4 Drama
- Reflect on how working in role helps to explore complex issues.

Read and write for a range of purposes on paper and on screen

Strand 6 Word structure and spelling
- Spell words containing unstressed vowels.
- Group and classify words according to their spelling patterns and their meanings.

Strand 7 Understanding and interpreting texts
- Make notes on and use evidence from across a text to explain events or ideas.
- Compare different types of narrative and information texts and identify how they are structured.

Strand 8 Engaging with and responding to texts
- Reflect on reading habits and preferences and plan personal reading goals.

Strand 9 Creating and shaping texts
- Reflect independently and critically on their own writing and edit and improve it.
- Adapt non-narrative forms and styles to write fiction or factual texts, including poems.
- Create multi-layered texts, including use of hyperlinks and linked web pages.

Strand 10 Text structure and organisation
- Experiment with the order of sections and paragraphs to achieve different effects.
- Change the order of material within a paragraph, moving the topic sentence.

Strand 11 Sentence structure and punctuation
- Adapt sentence construction to different text-types, purposes and readers.
- Punctuate sentences accurately, including using speech marks and apostrophes.

Strand 12 Presentation
- Adapt handwriting for specific purposes, for example printing, use of italics.
- Use a range of ICT programs to present texts, making informed choices about which electronic tools to use for different purposes.

Key aspects of learning

Enquiry
- Children will seek, interpret and use the answers to their questions as well as those of others in their activity throughout this unit.

---

100 LITERACY ASSESSMENT LESSONS · YEAR 5   ■ SCHOLASTIC

Key aspects of learning (contd)

Information processing
● Children will know where to find information and understand what is relevant and locate this within sources. They will use strategies such as skimming and scanning and using an index to locate information. They will identify the most relevant information from different sources and use this as a basis for writing.

Evaluation
● Children will compare and evaluate the effectiveness of recount text in a variety of forms. They will share their outcomes, discuss success criteria, give feedback to others and judge the effectiveness of their own work.

Communication
● Children will develop their ability to discuss effective and relevant communication in respect of both the form and the content of the non-fiction text they read or access and write or create. They will often work collaboratively in pairs and groups. They will communicate outcomes orally and in writing.

Assessment focuses

Reading
AF4 *(identify and comment on the structure and organisation of texts, including grammatical and presentational features at text level).*

Writing
AF2 *(produce texts which are appropriate to task, reader and purpose).*
AF7 *(select appropriate and effective vocabulary).*
AF8 *(use correct spelling).*

Speaking and listening
Speaking (adapt speech to audience; speak clearly).
Listening (understand and respond appropriately to feedback from peers and teacher).
Group discussion and interaction (include and respond to all members of the group; make contributions to sustain and complete the activity).
Drama (work in role; work with others).

Resources

Phase 1 activities
Photocopiable page, 'Questions'
Interactive activity, 'Open or closed questions?'
Photocopiable page, 'Occupations'
Interactive activity, 'Occupations'
Phase 2 activities
Photocopiable page, 'A legend honoured' (versions 1 and 2)
Interactive activity, 'Speech punctuation' (versions 1 and 2)
Photocopiable page, 'Alternatives for 'said'' (versions 1 and 2)
Interactive activity, 'Connectives' (versions 1 and 2)
Phase 3 and 4 activities
Photocopiable page, 'Research plan evaluation'
Periodic assessment
Interactive activity, 'Non-fiction 2 Reading assessment'

Unit 2 ▢ Recounts

Learning outcomes	Assessment opportunity and evidence	Assessment focuses (AFs)		Success criteria
		Level 2	Level 3	
Phase ① activities pages 119–120				
Questions Children demonstrate an understanding of the most effective questioning techniques to elicit high quality information.	• Supported group activity where children pick question cards and ask questions to elicit responses other than single-word answers. • Children's oral responses, notes made against the class list and group activity (photocopiable page).	**Reading AF4** • Some awareness of use of features of organisation.	**Reading AF4** • A few basic features of organisation at text level identified, with little or no linked comment.	• I can use effective questioning to gain information. • I can identify 'open' and 'closed' questions.
Suffixes and prefixes Children can spell words with less common suffixes.	• Independent activity where children choose the correct suffix for words describing occupations. • Children's completed activity on the photocopiable page.	**Writing AF8** • Usually correct spelling of: high frequency grammatical function words; common single morpheme content/lexical words. • Likely errors: inflected endings adverbs; phonetic attempts at vowel digraphs.	**Writing AF8** • Correct spelling of: some common grammatical function words; common content/lexical words with more than one morpheme, including compound words. • Likely errors: some inflected endings; some phonetically plausible attempts at content/lexical words.	I can spell words with less common suffixes.
Phase ② activities pages 121–124				
Features of a recount text Children can identify the features of the most successful recount text.	• Paired activity where children highlight the features of a recount text, swap pages, compare the features identified and give feedback. • Children's annotated notes on the photocopiable page and oral feedback.	**Reading AF4** • Some awareness of use of features of organisation.	**Reading AF4** • A few basic features of organisation at text level identified, with little or no linked comment.	I can identify the features that occur in good recount text.
Speech punctuation Children can understand the differences between the punctuation of reported and direct speech.	• Independent activity where children demonstrate an understanding of speech punctuation and describe how reported and direct speech punctuation differs. • Children's completed interactive activities, oral responses and notes against the class list.	**Reading AF4** • Some awareness of use of features of organisation.	**Reading AF4** • A few basic features of organisation at text level identified, with little or no linked comment.	I can punctuate direct and reported speech.
Synonyms for 'said' Children can use a variety of reporting clauses in dialogue and reported speech.	• Paired activity where children choose ways to report direct and indirect speech. • Children's written responses on the photocopiable page, paired feedback and notes against the class list.	**Writing AF7** • Simple, often speech-like vocabulary conveys relevant meanings. • Some adventurous word choices.	**Writing AF7** • Simple, generally appropriate vocabulary used, limited in range. • Some words selected for effect or occasion.	I can use other words and phrases to replace 'said'.

Unit 2 ▭ Recounts

Learning outcomes	Assessment opportunity and evidence	Assessment focuses (AFs)		Success criteria
		Level 2	**Level 3**	
Connecting paragraphs Children can write in paragraphs appropriately and use connectives well to improve the flow of writing.	● Independent activity where children choose connecting words to link paragraphs. ● Children's completed interactive activities and oral feedback.	**Writing AF7** ● Simple, often speech-like vocabulary conveys relevant meanings. ● Some adventurous word choices.	**Writing AF7** ● Simple, generally appropriate vocabulary used, limited in range. ● Some words selected for effect or occasion.	● I can write using paragraphs appropriately. ● I can improve the flow of writing by using connectives.

Phase ③ and ④ activity page 125

Learning outcomes	Assessment opportunity and evidence	Level 2	Level 3	Success criteria
Reviewing a plan ● Children can write a recount text using notes made from interviews. ● Children can use appropriate language and grammar. ● Children can evaluate a research plan.	● Supported group activity where children describe their own research plans, evaluate others' plans, edit and improve their own plans. ● Teacher observation, oral responses, notes against the class list and completed evaluations (photocopiable page).	**Writing AF2** ● Some basic purpose established. ● Some appropriate features of the given form used. ● Some attempts to adopt appropriate style.	**Writing AF2** ● Purpose established at a general level. ● Main features of selected form sometimes signalled to the reader. ● Some attempts at appropriate style, with attention to reader.	● I can use notes made from interviews to write a recount text. ● I can use appropriate language and grammar. ● I can evaluate a research plan.

Learning outcomes	Assessment opportunity and evidence	Assessment focuses (AFs)		Success criteria
		Level 4	**Level 5**	

Phase ① activities pages 119–120

Learning outcomes	Assessment opportunity and evidence	Level 4	Level 5	Success criteria
Questions Children demonstrate an understanding of the most effective questioning techniques to elicit high quality information.	● Supported group activity where children pick question cards and ask questions to elicit responses other than single-word answers. ● Children's oral responses, notes made against the class list and completed interactive activity.	**Reading AF4** ● Some structural choices identified with simple comment. ● Some basic features of organisation at text level identified.	**Reading AF4** ● Comments on structural choices show some general awareness of writer's craft. ● Various features relating to organisation at text level, including form, are clearly identified, with some explanation.	● I can use effective questioning to gain information. ● I can identify 'open' and 'closed' questions.
Suffixes and prefixes Children can spell words with less common suffixes.	● Independent activity where children choose the correct suffix for words describing occupations. ● Children's completed interactive activities.	**Writing AF8** ● Correct spelling of: most common grammatical function words, including adverbs with -ly formation; regularly formed content lexical words, including those with multiple morphemes; most past and present tense inflections, plurals. ● Likely errors: homophones of some common grammatical function words; occasional phonetically plausible spelling in content/lexical words.	**Writing AF8** ● Correct spelling of: grammatical function words; almost all inflected words; most derivational suffixes and prefixes; most content/lexical words. ● Likely errors: occasional phonetically plausible spelling of unstressed syllables in content words; double consonants in prefixes.	I can spell words with less common suffixes.

Unit 2 ⬜ Recounts

Learning outcomes	Assessment opportunity and evidence	Assessment focuses (AFs)		Success criteria
		Level 4	Level 5	
Phase ② activities pages 121–124				
Features of a recount text Children can identify the features of the most successful recount text.	● Paired activity where children highlight the features of a recount text, swap pages, compare the features identified and give feedback. ● Children's annotated notes on the photocopiable page and oral feedback.	**Reading AF4** ● Some structural choices identified with simple comment. ● Some basic features of organisation at text level identified.	**Reading AF4** ● Comments on structural choices show some general awareness of writer's craft. ● Various features relating to organisation at text level, including form, are clearly identified, with some explanation.	I can identify the features that occur in good recount text.
Speech punctuation Children can understand the differences between the punctuation of reported and direct speech.	● Independent activity where children demonstrate an understanding of speech punctuation and describe how reported and direct speech punctuation differs. ● Children's completed interactive activities, oral responses and notes against the class list.	**Reading AF4** ● Some structural choices identified with simple comment. ● Some basic features of organisation at text level identified.	**Reading AF4** ● Comments on structural choices show some general awareness of writer's craft. ● Various features relating to organisation at text level, including form, are clearly identified, with some explanation.	I can punctuate direct and reported speech.
Synonyms for 'said' Children can use a variety of reporting clauses in dialogue and reported speech.	● Paired activity where children choose ways to report direct and indirect speech. ● Children's written responses on photocopiable page, paired feedback and notes against the class list.	**Writing AF7** ● Some evidence of deliberate vocabulary choices. ● Some expansion of general vocabulary to match topic.	**Writing AF7** ● Vocabulary chosen for effect. ● Reasonably wide vocabulary used, though not always appropriately.	I can use other words and phrases to replace 'said'.
Connecting paragraphs Children can write in paragraphs appropriately and use connectives well to improve the flow of writing.	● Independent activity where children choose connecting words to link paragraphs. ● Children's completed interactive activities and oral feedback.	**Writing AF7** ● Some evidence of deliberate vocabulary choices. ● Some expansion of general vocabulary to match topic.	**Writing AF7** ● Vocabulary chosen for effect. ● Reasonably wide vocabulary used, though not always appropriately.	● I can write using paragraphs appropriately. ● I can improve the flow of writing by using connectives.
Phase ③ and ④ activity page 125				
Reviewing a plan ● Children can write a recount text using notes made from interviews. ● Children can use appropriate language and grammar. ● Children can evaluate a research plan.	● Group activity where children describe their own research plans, evaluate others' plans, edit and improve their own plans. ● Teacher observation, oral responses, notes against the class list and completed evaluations (photocopiable page).	**Writing AF2** ● Main purpose of writing is clear but not always consistently maintained. ● Main features of selected form are clear and appropriate to purpose. ● Style generally appropriate to task, though awareness of reader not always sustained.	**Writing AF2** ● Main purpose of writing is clear and consistently maintained. ● Features of selected form clearly established with some adaptation to purpose. ● Appropriate style clearly established to maintain reader's interest throughout.	● I can use notes made from interviews to write a recount text. ● I can use appropriate language and grammar. ● I can evaluate a research plan.

Phase ① Questions

Learning outcome
Children demonstrate an understanding of the most effective questioning techniques to elicit high quality information.

Success criteria
● I can use effective questioning to gain information.
● I can identify 'open' and 'closed' questions.

Setting the context
This assessment should be carried out once children have had the opportunity to view or listen to a recorded interview and discuss and make notes of the types of question used by the interviewer. They should have had the opportunity to use similar types of question in a hot-seat activity and explore which type of questions elicited the most comprehensive responses. Discuss the type of language used. Ask them to say which were the most successful questions. *What did they have in common?* Introduce the concept of 'open' and 'closed' questions, ie those that can have a simple 'yes', 'no', one-word or short-phrase response and those that invite the interviewee to expand their response.

Assessment opportunity
Invite children working at levels 4-5 to do the interactive activity 'Open or closed questions'. They will work independently to decide if a selection of questions are 'open' or 'closed'. Ask children working at levels 2-3 to work in a group using the cards from the photocopiable page 'Questions'. They should work in a supported group using the cut-out question cards from the photocopiable page. Children pick a card and use it to pose an open question. A supporting adult can make notes of their responses against the class list.

Assessment evidence
Children working at levels 2-3 recognise that questions beginning with inverted verbs such as 'Are you' or 'Do you' can elicit one-word responses and are 'closed'. They can identify some questions that are open. Children working at levels 4-5 are aware that how the question is phrased is important when asking open questions. Invite children to summarise the differences between 'open' and 'closed' questions. Use notes made against the class list, oral responses and the completed interactive or group activity to provide evidence against Reading AF4.

Next steps
Support: Ask children to work in pairs and ask each other questions that require answers of more than one word.
Extension: Invite children to write a selection of questions that would help them find out more about a famous personality, for example their favourite sports person or pop star.

Key aspects of learning
Enquiry: Children will seek, interpret and use the answers to their questions as well as those of others in their activity throughout this unit.
Communication: Children will develop their ability to discuss effective and relevant communication in respect of both the form and the content of the non-fiction text they read or access and write or create. They will often work collaboratively in pairs and groups. They will communicate outcomes orally and in writing.

NON-FICTION

Phase ① Suffixes and prefixes

Learning outcome
Children can spell words with less common suffixes.

Success criteria
I can spell words with less common suffixes.

Setting the context
This assessment should be carried out during phase 1 of this unit once children have explored different types of recount text in shared and guided reading, including biographies and autobiographies. Discuss the occupations and professions of the subjects of the autobiographies and biographies in the class or school library. Remind children that these titles are made by adding a suffix word to a root word. Invite children working at levels 4-5 to do the interactive activity 'Occupations', focusing on the spellings of titles of professions or occupations. Children working at levels 2-3 do the activity using the photocopiable page 'Occupations'.

Assessment opportunity
Children working at levels 2-3 sometimes confuse the 'er/or' endings. Children at levels 4-5 mostly identify the correct form of spelling in the names of professions. This activity provides the opportunity to assess children's knowledge of root words and the suffixes -cian, -tian, -ist, -or, and –er.

Assessment evidence
Use children's completed interactive activity and photocopiable pages to provide evidence against Writing AF8.

Next steps
Support: Ask children to practise spelling words they are unsure of using look, cover, write, check.
Extension: Invite children to collect names of other professions with unusual suffixes, for example, surgeon.

Key aspects of learning
Communication: Children will develop their ability to discuss effective and relevant communication in respect of both the form and the content of the non-fiction text they read or access and write or create. They will often work collaboratively in pairs and groups. They will communicate outcomes orally and in writing.

Phase ② Features of a recount text

Success criteria
I can identify the features that occur in good recount text.

Setting the context
This assessment activity should be undertaken once children have had opportunities to read and compare a variety of recount texts from different media such as newspapers, e-newspapers and magazines including some that make use of interviews. Through shared and guided reading, they should have had the opportunity to investigate and establish the key features, similarities and differences. Remind the children about recorded interviews they have seen or listened to and compare the key similarities and differences between oral and written recounts. Provide children with copies of the photocopiable page 'A legend honoured' (version 1 or 2) and ask them to mark up the features they have identified in shared and guided sessions. Children working at levels 2–3 should work with a partner using version 1 of the photocopiable page.

Assessment opportunity
This activity provides an opportunity to evaluate how secure children are in their knowledge of the layout and language features of recount text including the difference between reported and direct speech. Ask the children to highlight the features using different coloured pens, for example, past tense in blue, quotations in yellow, reported speech in green, changes in focus within paragraphs in pink. They should record any other features they notice. When they have finished, ask children to swap with a partner and compare the features they each identified. Take feedback and encourage children to say why they have highlighted certain features, with evidence from the text, and make notes of their responses against the class list.

Assessment evidence
Children working at levels 2–3 will identify past-tense verbs as being a clear indicator of recount text. Children at levels 4–5 will show an understanding of the reasons why text is grouped in paragraphs. Use children's annotated pages, oral feedback and notes made against the class list to provide evidence against Reading AF4.

Next steps
Support: Provide children with other texts cut out from newspapers and magazines and encourage them to highlight the features.
Extension: Invite children to discuss their annotated photocopiable pages in a group and use this as a basis for drawing up a list of features.

Key aspects of learning
Enquiry: Children will seek, interpret and use the answers to their questions as well as those of others in their activity throughout this unit.
Information processing: Children will know where to find information and understand what is relevant and locate this within sources. They will use strategies such as skimming and scanning and using an index to locate information. They will identify the most relevant information from different sources and use this as a basis for writing.
Evaluation: Children will compare and evaluate the effectiveness of recount text in a variety of forms. They will share their outcomes, discuss success criteria, give feedback to others and judge the effectiveness of their own work.
Communication: Children will develop their ability to discuss effective and relevant communication in respect of both the form and the content of the non-fiction text they read or access and write or create. They will often work collaboratively in pairs and groups. They will communicate outcomes orally and in writing.

NON-FICTION

Phase ② Speech punctuation

Learning outcome
Children can understand the differences between the punctuation of reported and direct speech.

Success criteria
I can punctuate direct and reported speech.

Setting the context
This assessment should be carried out when children have revised the conventions for punctuating speech from Year 4. They should have had the opportunity to investigate speech punctuation in recount text, such as newspaper reports, magazines and interviews, including examples of quotations and reported speech. Invite children working at levels 4-5 to complete version 2 of the interactive activity 'Speech punctuation' by typing in the missing punctuation marks. Invite children working at levels 2-3 to choose the correct punctuation marks from the drop-down box in version 1 of the interactive activity, 'Speech punctuation'.

Assessment opportunity
Once children have added the punctuation marks to the interactive activity, go through each screen with them and ask them to say which are direct speech, quotations or reported speech and describe how the punctuation is different. Make notes of their oral responses against the class list. Use this activity to evaluate how secure children are in their knowledge of punctuation in dialogue and other forms of written speech.

Assessment evidence
Children at all levels demonstrate they understand the use of inverted commas to denote the spoken words. Children at levels 2-3 sometimes choose the wrong option for ending a speech inside the final speech marks. Use children's oral and written evaluations to provide evidence against Reading AF4.

Next steps
Support: Provide children with recount texts from newspapers and magazines and two differently coloured highlighter pens. Ask them to go through the text and mark direct speech in one colour and reported speech in another.
Extension: Provide children with a recount text that includes direct and reported speech. Invite children to change the direct speech into reported speech and vice versa.

Key aspects of learning
Enquiry: Children will seek, interpret and use the answers to their questions as well as those of others in their activity throughout this unit.
Communication: Children will develop their ability to discuss effective and relevant communication in respect of both the form and the content of the non-fiction text they read or access and write or create. They will often work collaboratively in pairs and groups. They will communicate outcomes orally and in writing.

NON-FICTION

Phase ② Synonyms for 'said'

Success criteria
I can use other words and phrases to replace 'said'.

Setting the context
This assessment should be undertaken after the children have explored the uses of direct and reported speech in recount text in shared and guided reading. They should have identified verbs and reporting clauses used to describe speech and compared the differences in direct and reported speech. Ensure children are aware of the different purposes of using direct and reported speech in non-fiction texts and fiction writing. Invite children to complete the photocopiable page 'Alternatives for said' (versions 1 or 2) by choosing alternative words and phrases to replace the verb 'said' for each sentence. Children working at levels 2–3 will use version 1 of the photocopiable page.

Assessment opportunity
Invite children to swap their photocopiable pages with a partner and compare their choices of phrase with each other. Ask them to feed back which work best and how it changed the effect of using 'said' for the sentences.

Assessment evidence
Children working at levels 4–5 may use a variety of reporting clauses to replace 'said'. Children working at levels 2–3 are likely to rely on the choices in the box but do not make use of them all. Make notes against the class list of children's oral responses and use the completed photocopiable pages to provide evidence against Writing AF7.

Next steps
Support: Provide children with recount texts from newspapers and magazines and two differently coloured highlighter pens. Ask them to go through the text and mark the words and phrases used to report speech in different colours. Ask them to make a list of the most commonly used ones.
Extension: Provide children with a written conversation and ask them to read it aloud as reported speech.

Key aspects of learning
Evaluation: Children will compare and evaluate the effectiveness of recount text in a variety of forms. They will share their outcomes, discuss success criteria, give feedback to others and judge the effectiveness of their own work.
Communication: Children will develop their ability to discuss effective and relevant communication in respect of both the form and the content of the non-fiction text they read or access and write or create. They will often work collaboratively in pairs and groups. They will communicate outcomes orally and in writing.

Phase ② Connecting paragraphs

Learning outcome
Children can write in paragraphs appropriately and use connectives well to improve the flow of writing.

Success criteria
- I can write using paragraphs appropriately.
- I can improve the flow of writing by using connectives.

Setting the context
This assessment should be undertaken after the children have had experience in reading and analysing recount texts in shared and guided reading. They should have explored the use of paragraphs to change the focus of the information and revised the use of connectives to aid the flow of the writing. They should have had experience of experimenting with different connectives to link sentences and paragraphs in shared and guided writing. Invite children working at levels 4-5 to do version 2 of the interactive activity 'Connectives', choosing suitable connectives from their own knowledge to link information. Children working at levels 2-3 do version 1 of the interactive activity 'Connectives', choosing suitable connectives from the drop-down list.

Assessment opportunity
Use this activity as an opportunity to evaluate children's ability to use connectives to link paragraphs in a recount text. Invite the children to describe why they chose particular connectives and make notes against the class list.

Assessment evidence
Children working at levels 4-5 will generally score highly in the interactive activity. Use children's completed interactive activity to provide evidence against Writing AF7.

Next steps
Support: Ask children to use a thesaurus to identify other similar connecting words to use in their own writing.
Extension: Children re-read the text in the interactive activity and experiment with different connectives to find alternatives.

Key aspects of learning
Enquiry: Children will seek, interpret and use the answers to their questions as well as those of others in their activity throughout this unit.
Evaluation: Children will compare and evaluate the effectiveness of recount text in a variety of forms. They will share their outcomes, discuss success criteria, give feedback to others and judge the effectiveness of their own work.
Communication: Children will develop their ability to discuss effective and relevant communication in respect of both the form and the content of the non-fiction text they read or access and write or create. They will often work collaboratively in pairs and groups. They will communicate outcomes orally and in writing.

■SCHOLASTIC

Phase ③ and ④ Reviewing a plan

Learning outcomes
- Children can write a recount text using notes made from interviews.
- Children can use appropriate language and grammar.
- Children can evaluate a research plan.

Success criteria
- I can use notes made from interviews to write a recount text.
- I can use appropriate language and grammar.
- I can evaluate a research plan.

Setting the context
This assessment should be undertaken after the children have discussed a range of events that would lend themselves to be used as interviews for the class recount. They should have worked in groups to conduct interviews, make notes and analyse and interpret the information gained. They should have had experience of creating a research plan in modelled and shared writing, and have created their own research plans in groups. Children working at levels 2–3 should work with a supporting adult to discuss each other's plans and make notes. Display the success criteria in the classroom.

Assessment opportunity
Ask each group to describe their plan to the other groups. Observe and make notes against the class list. Invite the groups to make notes on the photocopiable page 'Research plan evaluation' to review and evaluate the plans of other groups by describing two things that will work well and one thing that could be worked on and improved. Invite them to give oral feedback to each group.

Assessment evidence
Children working at levels 2–3 identify simple aspects of the groups' descriptions of their plans such as the way they presented them orally rather than the content of the plans. Use observational notes and children's completed photocopiable pages to provide evidence against Writing AF2.

Next steps
Support: Invite groups to use the feedback evaluations to edit and improve their plans.
Extension: Invite groups to begin formulating ideas for the class recount using their research plans.

Key aspects of learning
Enquiry: Children will seek, interpret and use the answers to their questions as well as those of others in their activity throughout this unit.
Information processing: Children will know where to find information and understand what is relevant and locate this within sources. They will use strategies such as skimming and scanning and using an index to locate information. They will identify the most relevant information from different sources and use this as a basis for writing.
Evaluation: Children will compare and evaluate the effectiveness of recount text in a variety of forms. They will share their outcomes, discuss success criteria, give feedback to others and judge the effectiveness of their own work.
Communication: Children will develop their ability to discuss effective and relevant communication in respect of both the form and the content of the non-fiction text they read or access and write or create. They will often work collaboratively in pairs and groups. They will communicate outcomes orally and in writing.

Periodic assessment

Reading

Learning outcomes
- Children can identify the features of the most successful recount text.
- Children can understand the differences between the punctuation of reported and direct speech.

Success criteria
- I can recognise the features of recounts in different texts.
- I can identify the features that occur in good recount text.
- I can punctuate direct and reported speech.

Setting the context
Ensure children have read, compared and analysed a variety of different texts that include recounts. Invite them to do the interactive activity 'Non-fiction 2 Reading assessment' as a group. Children select 'true' or 'false' in response to statements about recount text. Encourage children to justify their answers by giving examples.

Assessment opportunity
Use the interactive activity and oral responses to assess children's confidence in their knowledge of the typical features of recount text. Make notes of individual children's responses against the class list.

Assessment evidence
Judge children's oral responses of their own achievements against your own observations during the unit and use this to provide judgements against Reading AF4 and AF5.

Writing

Learning outcomes
- Children can understand the differences between the punctuation of reported and direct speech.
- Children can use a variety of reporting clauses in dialogue and reported speech.
- Children can write a recount text using notes made from interviews.

Success criteria
- I can punctuate direct and reported speech.
- I can use other words and phrases to replace 'said'.
- I can write using paragraphs appropriately.
- I can improve the flow of writing using connectives.
- I can use notes made from interviews to write a recount text.

Setting the context
Collect the work that has been completed during the course of the unit and discuss individual children's achievements with them. Ask them to suggest what they found difficult about the work in the unit and what they found easy to accomplish. Make notes of their responses. Ask children to choose a piece of writing done at the beginning of the unit. Ask them to swap with a partner. Tell them to read their partner's work and describe what they think is needed to polish it. Invite them to revise their own writing, taking account of what they have learnt during the whole unit and their partner's comments.

Assessment opportunity
When children have added to or revised their recount texts, they swap them with their partners again. Invite the partners to evaluate what they have done to improve and polish the recount. This activity provides an opportunity to assess children's abilities to evaluate their own or another's writing.

Assessment evidence
Children's oral responses and their partner's evaluations of their completed recount text can be used to provide evidence against Writing AF3.

Name

Date

Occupations

■ Circle the word with the correct spelling. What are they?

1. A person who works in politics is a

| politician | politicion |

2. A person who sings is a

| singor | singer |

3. A person who performs magic tricks is a

| magician | magitian |

4. A person who drives is a

| driver | drivor |

5. A person who plays music is a

| musician | musicion |

6. A person who investigates is an

| investigator | investigater |

7. A person who treats sick people is a

| docter | doctor |

8. A person who writes novels is called a

| novelist | novellist |

Red
Amber
Green

I can spell words with less common suffixes.

Illustrations © Simon Smith/Beehive Illustration.

NON-FICTION
UNIT 3 Persuasive writing

Literacy objectives

Speak and listen for a wide range of purposes in different contexts
Strand 1 Speaking
- Present a spoken argument, sequencing points logically, defending views with evidence and making use of persuasive language.

Strand 2 Listening and responding
- Identify some aspects of talk that vary between formal and informal occasions.
- Analyse the use of persuasive language.

Strand 3 Group discussion and interaction
- Understand different ways to take the lead and support others in groups.
- Understand the process of decision making.

Strand 4 Drama
- Reflect on how working in role helps to explore complex issues.

Read and write for a range of purposes on paper and on screen
Strand 7 Understanding and interpreting texts
- Make notes on and use evidence from across a text to explain events or ideas.
- Infer writers' perspectives from what is written and from what is implied.
- Compare different types of narrative and information texts and identify how they are structured.
- Explore how writers use language for comic and dramatic effects.

Strand 9 Creating and shaping texts
- Reflect independently and critically on their own writing and edit and improve it.
- Create multi-layered texts, including use of hyperlinks and linked web pages.

Strand 10 Text structure and organisation
- Experiment with the order of sections and paragraphs to achieve different effects.
- Change the order of material within a paragraph, moving the topic sentence.

Strand 11 Sentence structure and punctuation
- Adapt sentence construction to different text-types, purposes and readers.
- Punctuate sentences accurately, including using speech marks and apostrophes.

Key aspects of learning

Enquiry
- Children will investigate how different persuasive texts influence the reader.

Information processing
- Children will evaluate a range of different persuasive texts that inform, protest or complain, and are able to analyse their language features.

Evaluation
- Children will collect and identify different persuasive devices and evaluate them for effectiveness.

Key aspects of learning (contd)

Reasoning
- Children will be able to give reasons for their opinions about the impact of a range of persuasive writing.

Communication
- Children will draft and write different persuasive texts for real purposes in pairs or individually.

Assessment focuses

Reading
AF5 *(explain and comment on writers' use of language, including grammatical and literary features at word and sentence level).*
AF6 *(identify and comment on writers' purposes and viewpoints, and the overall effect of the text on the reader).*

Writing
AF2 *(produce texts which are appropriate to task, reader and purpose).*
AF3 *(organise and present whole texts effectively, sequencing and structuring information, ideas and events).*
AF5 *(vary sentences for clarity, purpose and effect).*

Speaking and listening
Speaking (adapt to the audience; vary intonation and pace; use standard English).
Listening and responding (respond appropriately).
Group discussion and interaction (actively include and respond to all members of the group; take an active role in a group task over an extended period).
Drama (improvise and sustain role).

Resources

Phase 1 activities
Photocopiable page, 'Visit Venice!'
Photocopiable page, 'Persuasion'
Phase 2 activities
Photocopiable page, 'Persuasive language'
Interactive activity, 'Effective persuasion'
Photocopiable page, 'Letter of complaint' (versions 1 and 2)
Interactive activity, 'Sequencing a letter'
Phase 3 activities
Photocopiable page, 'The Piano film review'
Photocopiable page, 'Checklist for argument flyers'
Periodic assessment
Interactive activity, 'Non-fiction 3 Reading assessment'
Photocopiable page, 'Non-fiction 3 Writing assessment'

Unit 3 ☐ Persuasive writing

Learning outcomes	Assessment opportunity and evidence	Assessment focuses (AFs)		Success criteria
		Level 2	Level 3	
Phase ① activities pages 133-134				
What is persuasive writing? • Children can understand features of a persuasive text. • Children can identify phrases asserting a writer's point of view.	• Supported group activity where children discuss the features of a text. • Children's oral responses, notes made against the class list and completed photocopiable page.	**Reading AF5** • Some effective language choices noted. • Some familiar patterns of language identified.	**Reading AF5** • A few basic features of writer's use of language identified, but with little or no comment.	• I can analyse the use of persuasive writing. • I can understand writer's perspectives from what is written or implied.
Point of view Children can identify phrases asserting a writer's point of view.	• Paired activity where children present persuasive ideas. • Peer evaluation, notes made against the class list and children's written responses on the photocopiable page.	**Writing AF2** • Some basic purpose established. • Some appropriate features of the given form used. • Some attempts to adopt appropriate style.	**Writing AF2** • Purpose established at a general level. • Main features of selected form sometimes signalled to the reader. • Some attempts at appropriate style, with attention to reader.	• I can analyse the use of persuasive writing. • I can infer writer's perspectives from what is written or implied.
Phase ② activities pages 135-137				
Effective persuasion Children can understand how language is used for different purposes in persuasive texts.	• Paired activity where children categorise words and phrases by the emotions they evoke. • Children's interactive activity, oral responses and notes against the class list.	**Reading AF6** • Some awareness that writers have viewpoints and purposes. • Simple statements about likes and dislikes in reading, sometimes with reasons.	**Reading AF6** • Comments identify main purpose. • Express personal response but with little awareness of writer's viewpoint or effect on reader.	I can understand how writers use persuasive language for different effects.
A letter of complaint • Children can understand how language is used for different purposes in persuasive texts. • Children can develop a persuasive argument, using notes and feedback.	• Independent activity where children sequence a letter and make notes for a letter of complaint. • Children's completed interactive activity and notes made on the photocopiable page.	**Writing AF5** • Some variation in sentence openings. • Mainly simple sentences with *and* used to connect clauses. • Past and present tense generally consistent.	**Writing AF5** • Reliance mainly on simply structured sentences, variation with support. • *and, but, so* are the most common connectives, subordination occasionally. • Some limited variation in use of tense and verb forms, not always secure.	• I can understand how writers use persuasive language for different effects. • I can make notes to draft a persuasive text, sequencing points logically.
Ordering paragraphs Children can revise a letter by changing paragraphs and experimenting with order.	• Paired activity where children cut out and rearrange each other's letters to evaluate their writing. • Children's written outcomes and oral evaluations. Notes made against the class list.	**Writing AF3** • Some basic sequencing of ideas or material. • Openings and/or closings sometimes signalled.	**Writing AF3** • Some attempt to organise ideas with related points placed next to each other. • Openings and closings usually signalled. • Some attempt to sequence ideas or material logically.	I can experiment with the order of sections and paragraphs to achieve different effects.

Unit 3 ☐ Persuasive writing

Learning outcomes	Assessment opportunity and evidence	Assessment focuses (AFs)		Success criteria
		Level 2	Level 3	
Phase ③ activities page 138-139				
Reviewing a film Children can write a review of a film.	• Supported group activity where children write notes for a film review. • Children's oral responses and written notes on the photocopiable page.	**Writing AF2** • Some basic purpose established. • Some appropriate features of the given form used. • Some attempts to adopt appropriate style.	**Writing AF2** • Purpose established at a general level. • Main features of selected form sometimes signalled to the reader. • Some attempts at appropriate style, with attention to reader.	I can make notes and use evidence from a text to persuade others.
Writing an argument • Children can draft an argument, backed up with relevant information. • Children can create a flyer of their issue using a computer programme.	• Group activity where children evaluate each others' flyers about an issue, and give feedback. • Children's written responses on the photocopiable page and oral feedback.	**Writing AF2** • Some basic purpose established. • Some appropriate features of the given form used. • Some attempts to adopt appropriate style.	**Writing AF2** • Purpose established at a general level. • Main features of selected form sometimes signalled to the reader. • Some attempts at appropriate style, with attention to reader.	• I can make notes and use evidence from a text to persuade others. • I can experiment with the order of paragraphs to achieve different effects.

Learning outcomes	Assessment opportunity and evidence	Assessment focuses (AFs)		Success criteria
		Level 4	Level 5	
Phase ① activities pages 133-134				
What is persuasive writing? • Children can understand features of a persuasive text. • Children can identify phrases asserting a writer's point of view.	• Independent activity where children discuss the features of a text. • Children's oral responses and the completed photocopiable page.	**Reading AF5** • Some basic features of writer's use of language identified. • Simple comments on writer's choices.	**Reading AF5** • Various features of writer's use of language identified, with some explanation. • Comments show some awareness of the effect of writer's language choices.	• I can analyse the use of persuasive writing. • I can understand writer's perspectives from what is written or implied.
Point of view Children can identify phrases asserting a writer's point of view.	• Independent activity where children present persuasive ideas. • Peer evaluation, notes made against the class list and pupils' written outcomes.	**Writing AF2** • Main purpose of writing is clear but not always consistently maintained. • Main features of selected form are clear and appropriate to purpose. • Style generally appropriate to task, though awareness of reader not always sustained.	**Writing AF2** • Main purpose of writing is clear and consistently maintained. • Features of selected form clearly established with some adaptation to purpose. • Appropriate style clearly established to maintain reader's interest throughout.	• I can analyse the use of persuasive writing. • I can infer writer's perspectives from what is written or implied.

Unit 3 ☐ Persuasive writing

Learning outcomes	Assessment opportunity and evidence	Assessment focuses (AFs)		Success criteria
		Level 4	Level 5	
Phase ② activities pages 135-137				
Effective persuasion Children can understand how language is used for different purposes in persuasive texts.	• Independent activity where children categorise words and phrases by the emotions they evoke. • Children's interactive activity, oral responses and notes against the class list.	**Reading AF6** • Main purpose identified. • Simple comments show some awareness of writer's viewpoint. • Simple comments on overall effect on reader.	**Reading AF6** • Main purpose clearly identified often through general overview. • Viewpoint in texts clearly identified, with some, often limited, explanation. • General awareness of the effect on the reader, with some, often limited explanation.	I can understand how writers use persuasive language for different effects.
A letter of complaint Children can develop a persuasive argument, using notes and feedback.	• Independent activity where children sequence a letter and make notes for a letter of complaint. • Children's completed interactive activity and notes made on the photocopiable page.	**Writing AF5** • Some variety in length, structure or subject of sentences. • Use of some subordinating connectives. • Some variation, generally accurate, in tense and verb forms.	**Writing AF5** • A variety of sentence lengths, structures and subjects provides clarity and emphasis. • Wider range of connectives used to clarify relationship between ideas. • Some features of sentence structure used to build up detail or convey shades of meaning.	• I can understand how writers use persuasive language for different effects. • I can make notes to draft a persuasive text, sequencing points logically.
Ordering paragraphs Children can revise a letter by changing paragraphs and experimenting with order.	• Paired activity where children cut out and rearrange each other's letters to evaluate their writing. • Children's written outcomes and oral evaluations. Notes made against the class list.	**Writing AF3** • Ideas organised by clustering related points or by time sequence. • Ideas are organised simply with a fitting opening and closing, sometimes linked. • Ideas or material generally in logical sequence but overall direction of writing not always clearly signalled.	**Writing AF3** • Material is structured clearly, with sentences organised into appropriate paragraphs. • Development of material is effectively managed across text. • Overall direction of the text supported by clear links between paragraphs.	I can experiment with the order of sections and paragraphs to achieve different effects.
Phase ③ activities pages 138-139				
Reviewing a film Children can write a review of a film.	• Independent activity where children write notes for a film review. • Children's oral responses and written notes on the photocopiable page.	**Writing AF2** • Main purpose of writing is clear but not always consistently maintained. • Main features of selected form are clear and appropriate to purpose. • Style generally appropriate to task, though awareness of reader not always sustained.	**Writing AF2** • Main purpose of writing is clear and consistently maintained. • Features of selected form clearly established with some adaptation to purpose. • Appropriate style clearly established to maintain reader's interest throughout.	I can make notes and use evidence from a text to persuade others.
Writing an argument • Children can draft an argument, backed up with relevant information. • Children can create a flyer of their issue using a computer programme.	• Group activity where children independently evaluate each others' flyers about an issue, and give feedback. • Children's written outcomes and oral feedback.	**Writing AF2** • Main purpose of writing is clear but not always consistently maintained. • Main features of selected form are clear and appropriate to purpose. • Style generally appropriate to task, though awareness of reader not always sustained.	**Writing AF2** • Main purpose of writing is clear and consistently maintained. • Features of selected form clearly established with some adaptation to purpose. • Appropriate style clearly established to maintain reader's interest throughout.	• I can make notes and use evidence from a text to persuade others. • I can experiment with the order of paragraphs to achieve different effects.

Phase ① What is persuasive writing?

Learning outcomes
● Children can understand features of a persuasive text.
● Children can identify phrases asserting a writer's point of view.

Success criteria
● I can analyse the use of persuasive writing.
● I can understand writers' perspectives from what is written or implied.

Setting the context
This assessment should be carried out once children have had the opportunity to explore the language of persuasive texts on paper and on screen in shared, guided and independent reading. They should have explored the purposes of persuasive text, ie to make someone want to buy something or to act in a certain way. They should also have had opportunities to compare persuasive texts with texts that inform, looking at their similarities and differences. Invite children to identify persuasive features using the photocopiable page 'Visit Venice!'

Assessment opportunity
Children working at levels 4-5 will work independently to select the persuasive features. Children working at levels 2-3 work in a supported group and discuss the text before selecting their answers independently. An adult working with the group can make notes of their oral responses.

Assessment evidence
Children working at levels 2-3 can identify the questions and statistics in the text with help from an adult. They struggle to identify exaggerated language. Children working at levels 4-5 recognise the use of groups of three as a persuasive technique. They notice the alliterative use of 'renewed, refreshed and ready' as effective use of language. They recognise exaggerated language. Use notes made against the class list, oral responses and the completed photocopiable page to provide evidence against Reading AF5 (see also AF6).

Next steps
Support: Provide children with a clear list of the typical features of persuasive writing.
Extension: Invite children to identify and describe persuasive techniques seen when watching television at home.

Key aspects of learning
Enquiry: Children will investigate how different persuasive texts influence the reader.
Information processing: Children will evaluate a range of different persuasive texts that inform, protest or complain, and are able to analyse their language features.
Evaluation: Children will collect and identify different persuasive devices and evaluate them for effectiveness.

Phase ① Point of view

Learning outcome
Children can identify phrases asserting a writer's point of view.

Success criteria
● I can analyse the use of persuasive writing.
● I can infer writer's perspectives from what is written or implied.

Setting the context
This assessment activity should be undertaken once children have had opportunities to read and analyse writing that attempts to persuade the reader to change their point of view about an issue, during shared and guided reading. Remind the children that this type of persuasive text usually focuses on one side of an argument only. Provide the children with an issue to discuss, if possible one that affects them and has been discussed in other curriculum areas, for example, no chips for school dinners or school uniforms must be worn. Ask the children to take one viewpoint, either strongly in favour of or strongly against the issue, and make notes of persuasive arguments to change other people's minds using the photocopiable page 'Persuasion'. Children working at levels 2-3 should make notes on the photocopiable page with a partner, with both taking the same point of view.

Assessment opportunity
Invite pairs of children with contrasting opinions to read their notes aloud and ask others in the class to vote on which one was the most persuasive. Observe and make notes of children's oral contributions and evaluations.

Assessment evidence
Children working at levels 2-3 use some persuasive techniques, such as addressing the reader directly, but do not always sequence their points logically. Children working at levels 4-5 use connectives to sequence their points and use some emotive language. Use children's written notes and peer evaluation to provide evidence against Writing AF2.

Next steps
Support: For children who struggled to persuade others to their point of view, revisit their notes in a guided writing session to improve their points and the language they used.
Extension: Invite children to write their notes as a complete piece of persuasive writing, for example, a letter.

Key aspects of learning
Enquiry: Children will investigate how different persuasive texts influence the reader.
Evaluation: Children will collect and identify different persuasive devices and evaluate them for effectiveness.
Reasoning: Children will be able to give reasons for their opinions about the impact of a range of persuasive writing.
Communication: Children will draft and write different persuasive texts for real purposes in pairs or individually.

Phase ② Effective persuasion

Learning outcome

Children can understand how language is used for different purposes in persuasive texts.

Success criteria
I can understand how writers use persuasive language for different effects.

Setting the context
This assessment should be carried out after the children have had the opportunity to compare the effects of different words and phrases that writers use to create a reaction in persuasive writing. In shared and guided reading they should have explored emotive devices in a variety of persuasive texts written for different purposes, for example: to persuade people to buy something, to contribute to charity, to oppose new buildings, to change behaviour and so on. Invite the children to do the interactive activity 'Effective persuasion'. Explain that this is an unmarked activity and they should use their own opinions to categorise the examples. Children working at levels 2–3 should do the activity in pairs.

Assessment opportunity
This activity provides the opportunity to evaluate children's understanding of how a writer uses particular words and phrases in order to provoke a desired reaction. When children have completed the activity, ask them to describe the reasons for their choices and why the writers have wanted to achieve each of these reactions from readers. Make notes of their responses.

Assessment evidence
Children working at levels 2–3 may identify some phrases that fit the 'wishing, longing, envy' category. Children working at levels 4–5 may explain how shocking the reader can affect their response to an issue. Use children's oral responses and completed interactive activity to provide evidence for Reading AF6 (see also AF5).

Next steps
Support: Provide other words and phrases from texts read in the unit and ask children to group them using photocopiable page 'Persuasive language'.
Extension: Invite children to write words and phrases from their own reading on the photocopiable page 'Persuasive language'.

Key aspects of learning
Enquiry: Children will investigate how different persuasive texts influence the reader.
Information processing: Children will evaluate a range of different persuasive texts that inform, protest or complain, and are able to analyse their language features.
Evaluation: Children will collect and identify different persuasive devices and evaluate them for effectiveness.
Reasoning: Children will be able to give reasons for their opinions about the impact of a range of persuasive writing.

NON-FICTION

Phase ② A letter of complaint

Learning outcomes
● Children can understand how language is used for different purposes in persuasive texts.
● Children can develop a persuasive argument, using notes and feedback.

Success criteria
● I can understand how writers use persuasive language for different effects.
● I can make notes to draft a persuasive text, sequencing points logically.

Setting the context
This assessment should be undertaken after the children have used a writing frame or skeleton outline to make notes for persuasive texts for different purposes in modelled, shared and guided writing. They should have explored connectives and phrases used to link points in an argument. Invite children to do the interactive activity 'Sequencing a letter' before explaining that they are going to make brief notes for a letter to complain. Provide them with an issue that has relevance for them, for example, the loss of a crossing patrol outside their school or something similar. Ask them to use the photocopiable page 'Letter of complaint' (version 1 or 2) to make notes of reasons to support their complaint and words to link their points. Provide children working at levels 2–3 with version 1 of the photocopiable page, which provides them with connectives from which to choose.

Assessment opportunity
This activity provides an opportunity to assess children's ability to sequence points logically using connecting words and phrases to link them.

Assessment evidence
Children working at levels 4–5 demonstrate their ability to use a variety of connectives logically. Children at levels 2–3 select their connectives from the choices randomly. Use children's completed interactive activity and notes on the photocopiable page 'Letter of complaint' to provide evidence against Writing AF5.

Next steps
Support: Encourage children to make a collection of linking words and phrases in writing journals to use in persuasive texts.
Extension: Encourage children to use their notes to give an oral presentation of their letter to complain.

Key aspects of learning
Enquiry: Children will investigate how different persuasive texts influence the reader.
Information processing: Children will evaluate a range of different persuasive texts that inform, protest or complain, and are able to analyse their language features.
Evaluation: Children will collect and identify different persuasive devices and evaluate them for effectiveness.
Communication: Children will draft and write different persuasive texts for real purposes in pairs or individually.

SCHOLASTIC

Phase ② Ordering paragraphs

Learning outcome
Children can revise a letter by changing paragraphs and experimenting with order.

Success criteria
I can experiment with the order of sections and paragraphs to achieve different effects.

Setting the context
This assessment should be undertaken after the children have had experience of writing different types of persuasive texts through shared, guided and independent reading and writing. They should have had practice at drafting, writing and improving instructional persuasive texts written for a variety of purposes. Before beginning the activity, make copies of their letters to enable them to cut out and re-order them without losing the original. Explain to the children that they are going to revisit a complaint letter written during the course of the unit and experiment with the order of paragraphs. Invite children to work with a partner. Tell them to swap letters with their partner. They cut out the paragraphs and experiment with rearranging them to the best effect.

Assessment opportunity
Use this activity as an opportunity for children to evaluate their own and their partner's writing. Ask children to read their rearranged version of their letter and discuss if it has improved the letter. Ask them to feed back the result to you and you can use their oral responses to make notes against the class list. Ask questions to guide their evaluations, such as: *How has the new order changed the letter? Does the new order make the points clearer/more forceful?*

Assessment evidence
Children working at levels 2-3 make few changes to their partners' original letters and cannot give logical reasons for their re-ordering. Children at levels 4-5 can explain logical reasons for the changes they made. Use children's oral evaluations to provide evidence against Writing AF3.

Next steps
Support: Children revise their letter in the light of their partners' evaluations.
Extension: Children rewrite their letters and add two further paragraphs.

Key aspects of learning
Enquiry: Children will investigate how different persuasive texts influence the reader.
Information processing: Children will evaluate a range of different persuasive texts that inform, protest or complain, and are able to analyse their language features.
Evaluation: Children will collect and identify different persuasive devices and evaluate them for effectiveness.
Reasoning: Children will be able to give reasons for their opinions about the impact of a range of persuasive writing.
Communication: Children will draft and write different persuasive texts for real purposes in pairs or individually.

NON-FICTION

Phase ③ Reviewing a film

Learning outcome
Children can write a review of a film.

Success criteria
I can make notes and use evidence from a text to persuade others.

Setting the context
This assessment should be undertaken after the children have completed Narrative Unit 5. Remind children about the film *The Piano* by Aidan Gibbons, and show it to them again. Discuss the film and ask children to say what they enjoyed or did not like about it and why. Explain that this is personal opinion so there is no right or wrong answer. Explain that they are going to write a review of the film. Discuss the purpose of a film review, ie to persuade someone to watch it or dissuade someone from watching it. Provide children with copies of the photocopiable page 'The Piano film review' and ask them to make notes for a review of the film.

Assessment opportunity
This activity provides an opportunity for children to demonstrate the use of persuasive language in a film review. Children working at levels 2-3 work in a supported group. A supporting adult can ask questions to deepen and draw out children's opinions, for example: *At which point in the film did you notice this? What is the overall mood of the film? How will you describe it without telling readers too much?* An adult working with the group can make notes of their responses against the class list.

Assessment evidence
Children working at levels 2-3 write the review as their personal opinion without using persuasive language. Children at levels 4-5 use effective adjectives to influence the reader. Use children's oral responses and written film reviews to provide evidence against Writing AF2.

Next steps
Support: Children present their reviews orally, using their notes for others to evaluate. They can amend their notes in the light of others' comments.
Extension: Children use their notes to write a polished film review.

Key aspects of learning
Enquiry: Children will investigate how different persuasive texts influence the reader.
Information processing: Children will evaluate a range of different persuasive texts that inform, protest or complain, and are able to analyse their language features.
Evaluation: Children will collect and identify different persuasive devices and evaluate them for effectiveness.
Reasoning: Children will be able to give reasons for their opinions about the impact of a range of persuasive writing.
Communication: Children will draft and write different persuasive texts for real purposes in pairs or individually.

Phase ③ Writing an argument

Learning outcomes
● Children can draft an argument, backed up with relevant information.
● Children can create a flyer of their issue using a computer programme.

Success criteria
● I can make notes and use evidence from a text to persuade others.
● I can experiment with the order of paragraphs to achieve different effects.

Setting the context
This assessment should be undertaken after the children have worked in groups to explore issues that are relevant to their concerns and written an argument taking one point of view. They should have taken different roles and made notes for evidence to support different aspects of their argument and collaborated to arrange their information effectively. They should have had the opportunity to create a flyer about their issue using ICT. Explain that they are going to evaluate each group's flyer. Children working at levels 4–5 can make their notes independently. Provide children working at levels 2–3 with copies of the photocopiable page 'Checklist for argument flyers'. Invite children to view the persuasive flyers, making notes for each on the photocopiable page or independently, as appropriate.

Assessment opportunity
This activity provides an opportunity for children to demonstrate their knowledge of the use of persuasive language in arguments about an issue and their ability to apply that knowledge to their own writing and to evaluate it in the work of others. In a plenary session, invite children to give their prepared feedback to the groups by describing two aspects that worked well and one that could be worked on.

Assessment evidence
Judge children's evaluations of the persuasive techniques used in the flyers against your own assessments. Use children's oral responses and written notes to provide evidence against Writing AF2 (see also AF7).

Next steps
Support: Encourage the groups to edit and improve their flyers in the light of the feedback.
Extension: Groups should write another flyer on the same issue using a different style and compare their effectiveness.

Key aspects of learning
Enquiry: Children will investigate how different persuasive texts influence the reader.
Information processing: Children will evaluate a range of different persuasive texts that inform, protest or complain, and are able to analyse their language features.
Evaluation: Children will collect and identify different persuasive devices and evaluate them for effectiveness.
Reasoning: Children will be able to give reasons for their opinions about the impact of a range of persuasive writing.
Communication: Children will draft and write different persuasive texts for real purposes in pairs or individually.

NON-FICTION

Periodic assessment

Reading

Learning outcomes
● Children can understand features of a persuasive text.
● Children can understand how language is used for different purposes in persuasive texts.

Success criteria
● I can analyse the use of persuasive language.
● I can understand writers' perspectives from what is written or implied.
● I can understand how writers use persuasive language for different effects.
● I can identify features of persuasive texts.

Setting the context
Review the work that has been done during the course of this unit and discuss children's achievements with them. Invite them to summarise what they have learned about persuasive texts and make notes of their responses. Invite them to do the interactive activity 'Non-fiction 3 Reading assessment'.

Assessment opportunity
Use the interactive activity and children's oral responses to assess children's confidence in their knowledge of the typical language, layout and purposes of persuasive texts. Make notes of individual children's responses.

Assessment evidence
Children working at levels 4–5 will generally more in the interactive activity. Use children's responses to the interactive activity and oral responses to provide judgements against Reading AF5 and AF6.

Writing

Learning outcome
Children can develop a persuasive argument, using notes and feedback.

Success criteria
● I can make notes to draft a persuasive text, sequencing points logically.
● I can experiment with the order of sections and paragraphs to achieve different effects.
● I can create multi-layered texts, including the use of hyperlinks.

Setting the context
Ask children to choose a piece of persuasive writing done at the beginning of the unit. Ask them to swap with a partner. Tell them to read their partner's work and describe what they think is needed to polish it. Invite them to revise their own writing, taking account of what they have learned during the whole unit and their partner's comments.

Assessment opportunity
When children have added to or revised their persuasive writing, they should swap with their partners again. Invite the partners to evaluate what they have done to improve the writing. Invite children to use the photocopiable page 'Non-fiction 3 Writing assessment' to identify two pieces of work they are pleased with and one piece that needs working on.

Assessment evidence
Judge children's oral responses and their partner's evaluations of their completed instructions against your observations made in the course of the unit. Their responses and the photocopiable page can be used to provide evidence against Writing AF2, AF3 and AF4.

Name   Date

Visit Venice!

- Highlight the rhetorical questions in yellow.
- Circle the words or phrases that are repeated in groups of three in blue.
- Highlight the sentences that use statistics in green.
- Underline the examples of exaggerated language.

Visit Venice by train

Imagine a leisurely journey in luxurious surroundings.
Imagine watching a fascinating landscape slide past your window.
Imagine arriving in Venice, refreshed and delighted.
Wouldn't you want to begin your holiday like that?

TerrificTrainTravel.com will organise every aspect of your journey. You arrive renewed,

relaxed and ready to begin your Venetian adventure. What better way could there possibly be?

100% of our customers tell us they are delighted with our service.
89% of our customers travel with us every year! All our customers receive personal service!
Why not join them and start a holiday of a life time in style?

For a limited period only!
Book before 11th March and receive a complimentary travel pack.

Illustration © 2009, Simon Smith/Beehive Illustration.

Red   Amber   Green

I can analyse the use of persuasive writing. ☐
I can understand writer's perspectives from what is written or implied. ☐

POETRY
UNIT 1 Poetic style

Literacy objectives

Speak and listen for a wide range of purposes in different contexts
Strand 3 Group discussion and interaction
- Understand different ways to take the lead and support others in groups.

Strand 4 Drama
- Perform a scripted scene making use of dramatic conventions.

Read and write for a range of purposes on paper and on screen
Strand 7 Understanding and interpreting texts
- Make notes on and use evidence from across a text to explain events or ideas.
- Infer writers' perspectives from what is written and from what is implied.
- Explore how writers use language for comic and dramatic effects.

Strand 8 Engaging with and responding to texts
- Reflect on reading habits and preferences and plan personal reading goals.
- Compare the usefulness of techniques such as visualisation, prediction and empathy in exploring the meaning of texts.
- Compare how a common theme is presented in poetry, prose and other media.

Strand 9 Creating and shaping texts
- Reflect independently and critically on their own writing and edit and improve it.
- Adapt non-narrative forms and styles to write fiction or factual texts, including poems.

Strand 12 Presentation
- Adapt handwriting for specific purposes, for example printing, use of italics.
- Use a range of ICT programs to present texts, making informed choices about which electronic tools to use for different purposes.

Key aspects of learning

Evaluation
- Children will present information orally, through drama and in writing. They will discuss success criteria, give feedback to others and judge the effectiveness of their own work.

Self-awareness
- Children will discuss and reflect on their personal responses to the poems.

Communication
- Children will develop their skills to reflect critically on what they have seen and read. They will develop their ability to present a poem orally and reflect critically on their own and others' work.

SCHOLASTIC

Assessment focuses

Reading
AF3 (deduce, infer or interpret information, events or ideas from texts).
AF5 (explain and comment on writers' use of language, including grammatical and literary features at word and sentence level).
AF6 (identify and comment on writers' purposes and viewpoints, and the overall effect of the text on the reader).

Writing
AF1 (write imaginative, interesting and thoughtful texts).
AF3 (organise and present whole texts effectively, sequencing and structuring information, ideas and events).
AF5 (vary sentences for clarity, purpose and effect).
AF7 (select appropriate and effective vocabulary).

Speaking and listening
Group discussion and interaction (actively include and respond to all members of the group).
Drama (identify qualities of others' performance).

Resources

Phase 1 activities
Photocopiable page, 'An Owl Flew in My Bedroom Once'
Photocopiable page, 'The Lost Angels'
Photocopiable page, 'Responding to the poems' (versions 1 and 2)
Phase 2 activities
Photocopiable page, 'An Owl Flew in My Bedroom Once'
Photocopiable page, 'The Lost Angels'
Photocopiable page, 'Comparing the poems' (versions 1 and 2)
Periodic assessment
Interactive activity, 'Poetry 1 Reading assessment'

Unit 1 🔲 Poetic style

Learning outcomes	Assessment opportunity and evidence	Assessment focuses (AFs)		Success criteria
		Level 2	**Level 3**	
Phase ① activity page 147				
Poetic language • Children can record and explain their understanding of the imagery in a poem. • Children can identify and explain their preferences for certain phrases.	• Independent activity where children annotate and discuss two poems, and then fill in a response sheet. • Children's oral and written responses on the photocopiable page.	**Reading AF5** • Some effective language choices noted. • Some familiar patterns of language identified. **Reading AF3** • Simple, plausible inference about events and information, using evidence from text. • Comments based on textual cues, sometimes misunderstood.	**Reading AF5** • A few basic features of writer's use of language identified, but with little or no comment. **Reading AF3** • Straightforward inference based on a single point of reference in the text. • Responses to text show meaning established at a literal level or based on personal speculation.	• I can explain why an author chose particular words to express an idea. • I can identify metaphors and similes.
Phase ② activity page 148				
Preferences • Children can write a journal entry expressing preferences. • Children can identify similarities and differences in form and language features used.	• Group activity where children discuss and analyse two poems, make notes and write a journal entry about their preference. • Children's oral responses, notes on the photocopiable page and written journal responses.	**Reading AF5** • Some effective language choices noted. • Some familiar patterns of language identified. **Reading AF6** • Some awareness that writers have viewpoints and purposes. • Simple statements about likes and dislikes in reading, sometimes with reasons. **Writing AF3** • Some basic sequencing of ideas or material. • Openings and/or closings sometimes signalled.	**Reading AF5** • A few basic features of writer's use of language identified, but with little or no comment. **Reading AF6** • Comments identify main purpose. • Express personal response but with little awareness of writer's viewpoint or effect on reader. **Writing AF3** • Some attempt to organise ideas with related points placed next to each other. • Openings and closings usually signalled. • Some attempt to sequence ideas or material logically.	• I can respond to poems explaining preferences. • I can compare the structure and language of two poems by different writers.
Phase ③ activity page 149				
Writing poetry • Children can write their own poem using structure of their choice. • Children can refine their own poem and make a final copy for publication.	• Paired activity where children write a draft poem, give feedback to each other and refine their drafts. • Children's oral and written responses.	**Writing AF1** • Mostly relevant ideas and content, sometimes repetitive or sparse. • Some apt word choices create interest. **Writing AF5** • Some variation in sentence openings. • Mainly simple sentences with *and* used to connect clauses. • Past and present tense generally consistent. **Writing AF7** • Simple, often speech-like vocabulary conveys relevant meanings. • Some adventurous word choices.	**Writing AF1** • Some appropriate ideas and content included. • Some attempt to elaborate on basic information or events. **Writing AF5** • Reliance mainly on simply structured sentences, variation with support • *and, but, so* are the most common connectives, subordination occasionally. • Some limited variation in use of tense and verb forms, not always secure. **Writing AF7** • Simple, generally appropriate vocabulary used, limited in range. • Some words selected for effect or occasion.	• I can write my own poem selecting structure and content. • I can refine work for publication.

Unit 1 Poetic style

Learning outcomes	Assessment opportunity and evidence	Assessment focuses (AFs)		Success criteria
		Level 4	Level 5	
Phase ① activity page 147				
Poetic language • Children can record and explain their understanding of the imagery in a poem. • Children can identify and explain their preferences for certain phrases.	• Independent activity where children annotate and discuss two poems, and then fill in a response sheet. • Children's oral and written responses on the photocopiable page.	**Reading AF5** • Some basic features of writer's use of language identified. • Simple comments on writer's choices. **Reading AF3** • Comments make inferences based on evidence from different points in the text. • Inferences often correct, but comments are not always rooted securely in the text or repeat narrative or content.	**Reading AF5** • Various features of writer's use of language identified, with some explanation. • Comments show some awareness of the effect of writer's language choices. **Reading AF3** • Comments develop explanation of inferred meanings drawing on evidence across the text. • Comments make inferences and deductions based on textual evidence.	• I can explain why an author chose particular words to express an idea. • I can identify metaphors and similes.
Phase ② activity page 148				
Preferences • Children can write a journal entry expressing preferences. • Children can identify similarities and differences in form and language features used.	• Group activity where children discuss and analyse two poems, make notes and write a journal entry about their preference. • Children's oral responses, notes on the photocopiable page and written journal responses.	**Reading AF5** • Some basic features of writer's use of language identified. • Simple comments on writer's choices. **Reading AF6** • Main purpose identified. • Simple comments show some awareness of writer's viewpoint. • Simple comment on overall effect on reader. **Writing AF3** • Ideas organised by clustering related points or by time sequence. • Ideas are organised simply with a fitting opening and closing, sometimes linked. • Ideas or material generally in logical sequence but overall direction of writing not always clearly signalled.	**Reading AF5** • Various features of writer's use of language identified, with some explanation. • Comments show some awareness of the effect of writer's language choices. **Reading AF6** • Main purpose clearly identified, often through general overview. • Viewpoint in texts clearly identified, with some, often limited, explanation. • General awareness of effect on the reader, with some, often limited, explanation. **Writing AF3** • Material is structured clearly, with sentences organised into appropriate paragraphs. • Development of material is effectively managed across text. • Overall direction of the text supported by clear links between paragraphs.	• I can respond to poems explaining preferences. • I can compare the structure and language of two poems by different writers.

Unit 1 ▢ Poetic style

Learning outcomes	Assessment opportunity and evidence	Assessment focuses (AFs)		Success criteria
		Level 4	Level 5	
Phase ③ activity page 149				
Writing poetry ● Children can write their own poem using structure of their choice. ● Children can refine their own poem and make a final copy for publication.	● Paired activity where children write a draft poem, give feedback to each other and refine their drafts. ● Children's oral and written responses.	**Writing AF1** ● Relevant ideas and content chosen. ● Some ideas and material developed in detail. **Writing AF5** ● Some variety in length, structure or subject of sentences. ● Use of some subordinating connectives, throughout the text. ● Some variation, generally accurate, in tense and verb forms. **Writing AF7** ● Some evidence of deliberate vocabulary choices. ● Some expansion of general vocabulary to match topic.	**Writing AF1** ● Relevant ideas and material developed with some imaginative detail. ● Development of ideas and material appropriately shaped for selected form. **Writing AF5** ● A variety of sentence lengths, structures and subjects provides clarity and emphasis. ● Wider range of connectives used to clarify relationship between ideas. ● Some features of sentence structure used to build up detail or convey shades of meaning. **Writing AF7** ● Vocabulary chosen for effect. ● Reasonably wide vocabulary used, though not always appropriately.	● I can write my own poem selecting structure and content. ● I can refine work for publication.

Phase ① Poetic language

Learning outcomes
● Children can record and explain their understanding of the imagery in a poem.
● Children can identify and explain their preferences for certain phrases.

Success criteria
● I can explain why an author chose particular words to express an idea.
● I can identify metaphors and similes.

Setting the context
This assessment should be carried out once children have explored and compared the use of poetic language, metaphor and simile, in the work of two contrasting poets. Ensure children have an understanding of the terms 'metaphor' and 'simile' and can identify both in the poetry that has been studied during the course of the first phase of this unit. Provide children with copies of the poems on the photocopiable pages, 'An Owl flew in My Bedroom Once' a poem by Jan Dean, and 'The Lost Angels' a poem by Brian Moses. Explain that they are to read both poems independently, annotate the poems to identify any poetic devices they recognise and answer the questions about the poems on the photocopiable page 'Responding to the poems' (version 1 or 2). Children working at levels 2-3 should use version 1 of the photocopiable page.

Assessment opportunity
Children will work independently on the two poems and identify any metaphors and similes, marking them on the sheets. They then answer the questions on the photocopiable page 'Responding to the poems' (version 1 or 2). Draw out and deepen children's responses orally by asking them to describe how each poem makes them feel and to identify any striking images or use of language giving reasons and quoting evidence from the poems.

Assessment evidence
Children working at levels 2-3 can explain which poem they prefer, referring to striking images in the text, for example: 'a piece of night adrift'. Children working at levels 4-5 can refer to the overall effect of the poem as a whole, for example: 'it makes you wonder if it was only the poet's imagination'. Children's annotated poems and written responses on the photocopiable page 'Responding to the poems' will provide evidence for Reading AF5. Notes made against the class list can provide evidence against Reading AF3.

Next steps
Support: For those children who need extra help in recognising metaphor and simile, provide other poems and ask them to find comparisons that use 'like/as' and those that do not.
Extension: Identify the use of simile and metaphor in another poem and compare the effect with the two poems from this activity.

Key aspects of learning
Evaluation: Children will present information orally, through drama and in writing. They will discuss success criteria, give feedback to others and judge the effectiveness of their own work.
Self-awareness: Children will discuss and reflect on their personal responses to the poems.
Communication: Children will develop their skills to reflect critically on what they have seen and read. They will develop their ability to present a poem orally and reflect critically on their own and others' work.

POETRY

Phase ② Preferences

Learning outcomes
● Children can write a journal entry expressing preferences.
● Children can identify similarities and differences in form and language features used.

Success criteria
● I can respond to poems explaining preferences.
● I can compare the structure and language of two poems by different writers.

Setting the context
This assessment activity should be undertaken once children have explored how poets use similar and varied structures to write poems and how these have different effects on readers, during phase two of this unit. Provide the children with copies of the poems on the photocopiable pages, 'An Owl flew in My Bedroom Once', a poem by Jan Dean, and 'The Lost Angels' a poem by Brian Moses. Ask them to work in small groups of similar ability. Allow them time to read, analyse and discuss the form of each poem, looking for unusual imagery, use of rhyme, metaphor and simile. Provide them with copies of the photocopiable page 'Comparing the poems' (version 1 or 2) and invite them to make notes about the first poem before adding notes about the second poem. (They may need to use extra paper.) They can then use their notes to write a journal entry, explaining their preferences. Children working at levels 2–3 should use version 1 of the photocopiable page 'Comparing the poems'.

Assessment opportunity
Children should be given sufficient time to read the poems, to digest them and to decide which they liked best and why. In small discussion groups of similar ability, children should express their preferences and explain their reasons. Observe children and use questioning to encourage extra depth. Record their comments against the class list. Questions might include: *What are both poems recounting? Does either poem use repetition or rhyme? Both poems end with an afterthought – what effect does this have in each poem? Why do you think Jan Dean/Brian Moses wrote the poem? Can you find an unusual image in each poem? Which image do you prefer and why?*

Assessment evidence
Record which children could express their preferences clearly giving reasons and who could identify unusual images such as 'a piece of night adrift' or 'creatures with angels' wings'. Use these comments to provide evidence against Reading AF5 and AF6. Their written journal responses will provide evidence for Writing AF3.

Next steps
Support: For children who struggled to recognise unusual imagery, choose appropriate poems to send home along with questions to lead them to analyse the poem, for example, 'The Magic Box' by Kit Wright or 'A Feather from an Angel' by Brian Moses.
Extension: Select a poem each week for children to take home, read and analyse and then to share and discuss in class. Keep this up as a regular end-of-week or start-to-the week activity.

Key aspects of learning
Self-awareness: Children will discuss and reflect on their personal responses to the poems.
Communication: Children will develop their skills to reflect critically on what they have seen and read. They will develop their ability to present a poem orally and reflect critically on their own and others' work.

SCHOLASTIC

Phase ③ Writing poetry

Learning outcomes
- Children can write their own poem using structure of their choice.
- Children can refine their own poem and make a final copy for publication.

Success criteria
- I can write my own poem, selecting structure and content.
- I can refine work for publication.

Setting the context
This assessment should be carried out after the children have completed the unit on poetic style. They should have examined a variety of poems that use varied structures and styles and explored the use of imagery, metaphor and simile. They should have created poems collaboratively in group or whole-class situations through shared and guided writing. Invite children to choose a form based on the work they have explored during the unit and a topic. Then ask them to create a first draft of their own individual poem.

Assessment opportunity
Children should share their drafts with a partner and evaluate each other's work. Ask them to identify two features of their partner's poem that work well and one feature for improvement. Using their peer feedback, ask children to improve their poems before writing a final version.

Assessment evidence
Children read their poems aloud and explain what improvements they made based on peer feedback and what effect this had on their own poems. Judge children's peer assessments against your own observations. Children working at levels 2-3 might include some interesting choices of similes or adjectives. Children working at levels 4-5 have made good attempts to write metaphors. Use children's final poems to provide evidence against Writing AF1. Use notes made against the class list of children's oral responses to provide evidence against Writing AF5 and AF7.

Next steps
Support: Encourage children to use the form and theme of poems they have read as models for their own writing, for example, poems about observation such as 'The Lost Angels' by Brian Moses.
Extension: Encourage children to write other poems in the same style and theme to create thematic anthologies for the class.

Key aspects of learning
Evaluation: Children will present information orally, through drama and in writing. They will discuss success criteria, give feedback to others and judge the effectiveness of their own work.
Self-awareness: Children will discuss and reflect on their personal responses to the poems.
Communication: Children will develop their skills to reflect critically on what they have seen and read. They will develop their ability to present a poem orally and reflect critically on their own and others' work.

POETRY

Periodic assessment

Reading

Learning outcomes
- Children can record and explain their understanding of the imagery in a poem.
- Children can identify similarities and differences in form and language features used.
- Children can understand the different structures used for different poems.

Success criteria
- I can identify and create metaphors and similes.
- I can identify how particular words are chosen for their precise meaning.
- I can identify different structures used by poets.

Setting the context
This assessment should be carried out once children have completed Poetry Unit 1. Ensure children have had experience of reading and analysing poems in shared and guided reading. Children should have an understanding of poetic imagery, metaphor and simile, and have had experience of rhyming and non-rhyming poetry, free verse and other forms of poetry. Review the poetry read during the work on this unit and ask children to comment on which poems they preferred, giving reasons for their choices. Encourage them to use the terms they have learnt to describe why they like particular poems, such as imagery, rhyme, metaphor and simile.

Assessment opportunity
Children should work independently using the interactive activity 'Poetry 1 Reading assessment'. They answer questions to identify a variety of different poetic features and forms of poetry in a drag-and-drop activity. This activity provides an opportunity to assess children's understanding of a wide variety of the features of poetry.

Assessment evidence
Children working at levels 4-5 should score highly on the interactive activity. At all levels, the children's completed interactive activity and notes made against the class list of oral responses can be used to provide judgements against Reading AF4.

Periodic assessment

Writing

Learning outcome
Children can write a journal entry expressing preferences.

Success criteria
● I can analyse and write my own poems, using poetic structures and techniques.
● I can respond to poems, explaining my preferences.

Setting the context
This assessment should be carried out once children have completed Poetry Unit 1. Ensure children have had experience of reading, writing and analysing poems in shared and guided reading and writing. Children should have an understanding of poetic imagery, metaphor and simile, and have had experience of rhyming and non-rhyming poetry, free verse and other forms of poetry. Collect the work that has been completed during the course of Unit 1 and discuss individual children's achievements with them. Ask them to suggest what they found difficult about the work in the unit and what they found easy to accomplish. Ask children to choose the poem written in the course of the work in this unit that they like the best. It can be a collaborative poem, one of the child's own poems or one written by another child. Invite them to annotate the poem to show the poetic features and form used and then to write a journal entry to explain why they prefer this poem.

Assessment opportunity
This activity provides an opportunity to assess children's abilities to evaluate their own or another's poetry writing and to give reasons for their opinion based on analysis of the form and features and to provide an explanation of their preference. It enables you to evaluate their understanding of the work covered in the whole unit.

Assessment evidence
Children working at levels 2-3 identify good use of rhyme and interesting choices of imagery. Children working at levels 4-5 can comment on the overall effect of the poem. At all levels, the children's completed journal entries can be used to provide judgements against Writing AF3.

An Owl Flew in My Bedroom Once

My attic bedroom had two windows –
One that opened high above the street
And a skylight – a tile of thick glass
Like a see-through slate.
And through it fell the moonlight
Coring the darkness like an apple-peeler.
Suddenly in that long cylinder of light
Appeared the owl, mysterious and grey
In that cold moon.
He flew in silently – a piece of night adrift –
Escaped. He circled, didn't settle
On the banister or rail.
There was no rattle of his talons,
No gripe or stomp
To make him solid with their sound,
He simply floated in – turned wide – and floated out...
In the morning there was nothing
No down or limy dropping
Nothing to prove he'd ever been at all.

An owl flew in my bedroom once, I think.

Jan Dean

The Lost Angels

In a fish tank in France
we discovered the lost angels,
fallen from heaven and floating now
on imaginary tides.
And all along the sides of the tank,
faces peered, leered at them,
laughing, pouting,
pointing, shouting,
while hung above their heads, a sign,
'Ne pas plonger les mains dans le basin.'
Don't put your hands in the tank
– the turtles bite seriously.
And who can blame them,
these creatures with angels' wings,
drifting past like alien craft.
Who knows what signals they send
through an imitation ocean,
out of sight of sky,
out of touch with stars?

Dream on, lost angels,
then one day, one glorious day,
you'll flap your wings
and fly again.

Brian Moses

POETRY

Name

Date

Responding to the poems (1)

■ Answer these questions about 'An Owl Flew in My Bedroom Once' by Jan Dean and 'The Lost Angels' by Brian Moses.

1. 'An Owl Flew in My Bedroom Once'. Write one sentence to say what the poem is about.

_____

_____

2. 'The Lost Angels'. Write one sentence to say what the poem is about.

_____

_____

3. Write a simile from 'The Lost Angels'.

_____

_____

4. Write one metaphor from 'An Owl Flew in My Bedroom Once'.

_____

_____

5. Which poem do you prefer? Give a reason for your answer.

_____

_____

_____

_____

Red
Amber
Green

I can explain why an author chose particular words to express an idea. ☐

I can identify metaphors and similes. ☐

Name   Date

Comparing the poems (1)

■ Compare the two poems and make notes about them in the columns.

	'An Owl Flew in My Bedroom Once'	'The Lost Angels'
What is the poem about?		
Language features		
I prefer...		

Red
Amber
Green

I can respond to poems explaining preferences. ☐

I can compare the structure and language of two poems by different writers. ☐

POETRY
UNIT 2 Narrative poetry

Literacy objectives

Speak and listen for a wide range of purposes in different contexts

Strand 3 Group discussion and interaction
- Plan and manage a group task over time using different levels of planning.
- Understand different ways to take the lead and support others in groups.
- Understand the process of decision making.

Strand 4 Drama
- Reflect on how working in role helps to explore complex issues.
- Use and recognise the impact of theatrical effects in drama.

Read and write for a range of purposes on paper and on screen

Strand 6 Word structure and spelling
- Spell words containing unstressed vowels.
- Group and classify words according to their spelling patterns and their meanings.

Strand 7 Understanding and interpreting texts
- Make notes on and use evidence from across a text to explain events or ideas.
- Explore how writers use language for comic and dramatic effects.

Strand 8 Engaging and responding to texts
- Compare how a common theme is presented in poetry, prose and other media.

Strand 12 Presentation
- Use a range of ICT programs to present texts, making informed choices about which electronic tools to use for different purposes.

Key aspects of learning

Enquiry
- Children will investigate an older narrative poem, seeking the answers to their own and others' questions. They will engage in drama and discussion and then plan and present their own version orally and visually.

Information processing
- Children will identify relevant information from a range of sources and use this as a basis for a choral performance of their own version of the poem.

Evaluation
- Children will present information orally, through drama and in writing. They will discuss success criteria, give feedback to others and judge the effectiveness of their own work.

Self-awareness
- Children will discuss and reflect on their personal responses to the poems.

Communication
- Children will develop their skills to reflect critically on what they have seen and read. They will develop their ability to present a poem orally and reflect critically on their own and others' work.

Assessment focuses

Reading

AF3 *(deduce, infer or interpret information, events or ideas from texts).*
AF5 *(explain and comment on writers' use of language, including grammatical and literary features at word and sentence level).*
AF6 *(identify and comment on writers' purposes and viewpoints, and the overall effect of the text on the reader).*
AF7 *(relate texts to their social, cultural and historical contexts and literary traditions).*

Writing

AF1 *(write imaginative, interesting and thoughtful texts).*
AF7 *(select appropriate and effective vocabulary).*

Speaking and listening

Group discussion and interaction (actively include and respond to all members of the group).
Drama (identify qualities of others' performance).

Resources

Phase 1 activities
Photocopiable page, 'Poetic devices' (versions 1 and 2)
Phase 2 activities
Photocopiable page, 'Character cards'
Recommended texts
'The Highwayman' by Alfred Noyes
'The Visitor' by Ian Serraillier
'The Song of Hiawatha' by Henry Wadsworth Longfellow
'The Bumblebee' by Nic Toczek
'The Listeners' by Walter de la Mare
Periodic assessment
Interactive activity, 'Poetry 2 Reading assessment'

Unit 2 ◻ Narrative poetry

Learning outcomes	Assessment opportunity and evidence	Assessment focuses (AFs)		Success criteria
		Level 2	Level 3	

Phase ① activity page 161

Learning outcomes	Assessment opportunity and evidence	Level 2	Level 3	Success criteria
Language and imagery Children understand the differences between literal and figurative language and can use the text to explain the effects of imagery in a poem.	• Independent activity where children read a narrative poem and identify poetic devices used. • Children's oral responses and written responses on the photocopiable page.	**Reading AF5** • Some effective language choices noted. • Some familiar patterns of language identified.	**Reading AF5** • A few basic features of writer's use of language identified, but with little or no comment.	• I can explore the effects of the vocabulary used in the text. • I can identify poetic techniques used to create tension.

Phase ② activity page 162

Learning outcomes	Assessment opportunity and evidence	Level 2	Level 3	Success criteria
First person • Children use their understanding of characters, language and plot to write in the first person. • Children can reflect on how working in role helps to explore some of the complex issues within a poem.	• Paired and group activity where children devise three questions to ask a character and sit in the hot seat in role before writing a first-person diary entry. • Children's oral and written responses.	**Reading AF3** • Simple, plausible inference about events and information, using evidence from text. • Comments based on textual cues, sometimes misunderstood. **Reading AF6** • Some awareness that writers have viewpoints and purposes. • Simple statements about likes and dislikes in reading, sometimes with reasons. **Reading AF7** • General features of a few text types identified. • Some awareness that books are set in different times and places. **Writing AF1** • Mostly relevant ideas and content, sometimes repetitive or sparse. • Some apt word choices create interest. • Brief comments, questions about events or actions suggest viewpoint. **Writing AF7** • Simple, often speech-like vocabulary conveys relevant meanings. • Some adventurous word choices.	**Reading AF3** • Straightforward inference based on a single point of reference in the text. • Responses to text show meaning established at a literal level or based on personal speculation. **Reading AF6** • Comments identify main purpose. • Express personal response but with little awareness of writer's viewpoint or effect on reader. **Reading AF7** • Some simple connections between texts identified. • Recognition of some features of the context of texts. **Writing AF1** • Some appropriate ideas and content included. • Some attempt to elaborate on basic information or events. • Attempt to adopt viewpoint, though often not maintained or inconsistent. **Writing AF7** • Simple, generally appropriate vocabulary used, limited in range. • Some words selected for effect or occasion.	• I can record opinions or thoughts about events in the poem in a first-person diary account. • I can work in role to infer or deduce ideas about character.

Phase ③ activity page 163

Learning outcomes	Assessment opportunity and evidence	Level 2	Level 3	Success criteria
Group performance Children demonstrate that they can work as a member of a group to plan, perform and evaluate a choral performance of a poem.	• Paired activity where children perform a group presentation of selected parts of a narrative poem. • Paired evaluation. Oral and written feedback.	**Reading AF7** • General features of a few text types identified. • Some awareness that books are set in different times and places.	**Reading AF7** • Some simple connections between texts identified. • Recognition of some features of the context of texts.	• I can understand different ways to take the lead and support others in the group. • I can evaluate my own work according to agreed criteria.

Unit 2 ▢ Narrative poetry

Learning outcomes	Assessment opportunity and evidence	Assessment focuses (AFs)		Success criteria
		Level 4	Level 5	

Phase ① activity page 161

Learning outcomes	Assessment opportunity and evidence	Level 4	Level 5	Success criteria
Language and imagery Children understand the differences between literal and figurative language and can use the text to explain the effects of imagery in a poem.	• Independent activity where children read a narrative poem and identify poetic devices used. • Children's oral responses and written responses on the photocopiable page.	**Reading AF5** • Some basic features of writer's use of language identified. • Simple comments on writer's choices.	**Reading AF5** • Various features of writer's use of language identified, with some explanation. • Comments show some awareness of the effect of writer's language choices.	• I can explore the effects of the vocabulary used in the text. • I can identify poetic techniques used to create tension.

Phase ② activity page 162

Learning outcomes	Assessment opportunity and evidence	Level 4	Level 5	Success criteria
First person • Children use their understanding of characters, language and plot to write in the first person. • Children can reflect on how working in role helps to explore some of the complex issues within a poem.	• Paired and group activity where children devise three questions to ask a character and sit in the hot seat in role before writing a first-person diary entry. • Children's oral and written responses.	**Reading AF3** • Comments make inferences based on evidence from different points in the text. • Inferences often correct, but comments are not always rooted securely in the text or repeat narrative or content. **Reading AF6** • Main purpose identified. • Simple comments show some awareness of writer's viewpoint. • Simple comment on overall effect on reader. **Reading AF7** • Features common to different texts or versions of the same text identified, with simple comment. • Simple comment on the effect that the reader's or writer's context has on the meaning of texts. **Writing AF1** • Relevant ideas and content chosen. • Some ideas and material developed in detail. • Straightforward viewpoint generally established and maintained. **Writing AF7** • Some evidence of Deliberate vocabulary choices. • Some expansion of general vocabulary to match topic.	**Reading AF3** • Comments develop explanation of inferred meanings drawing on evidence across the text. • Comments make inferences and deductions based on textual evidence. **Reading AF6** • Main purpose clearly identified, often through general overview. • Viewpoint in texts clearly identified, with some, often limited, explanation. • General awareness of effect on the reader, with some, often limited, explanation. **Reading AF7** • Comments identify similarities and differences between texts, or versions, with some explanation. • Some explanation of how the contexts in which texts are written and read contribute to meaning. **Writing AF1** • Relevant ideas and material developed with some imaginative detail • Development of ideas and material appropriately shaped for selected form. • Clear viewpoint established, generally consistent, with some elaboration. **Writing AF7** • Vocabulary chosen for effect • Reasonably wide vocabulary used, though not always appropriately.	• I can record opinions or thoughts about events in the poem in a first-person diary account. • I can work in role to infer or deduce ideas about character.

Unit 2 ⬜ Narrative poetry

Learning outcomes	Assessment opportunity and evidence	Assessment focuses (AFs)		Success criteria
		Level 4	Level 5	
Phase ③ activity pages 163				
Group performance Children demonstrate that they can work as a member of a group to plan, perform and evaluate a choral performance of a poem.	● Paired activity where children perform a group presentation of selected parts of a narrative poem. ● Paired evaluation. Oral and written feedback.	**Reading AF7** ● Features common to different texts or versions of the same text identified, with simple comment. ● Simple comment on the effect that the reader's or writer's context has on the meaning of texts.	**Reading AF7** ● Comments identify similarities and differences between texts, or versions, with some explanation. ● Some explanation of how the contexts in which texts are written and read contribute to meaning.	● I can understand different ways to take the lead and support others in the group. ● I can evaluate my own work according to agreed criteria.

Phase ① Language and imagery

Learning outcome
Children understand the differences between literal and figurative language and can use the text to explain the effects of imagery in a poem.

Success criteria
- I can explore the effects of the vocabulary used in the text.
- I can identify poetic techniques used to create tension.

Setting the context
This assessment should be carried out once children have explored and compared the use of language in classic narrative poems. Poems suitable for this activity include 'The Highwayman' by Alfred Noyes (available on the PNS website) or 'The Visitor' by Ian Serraillier. Ensure that children have an understanding of the terms 'metaphor', 'simile' and 'onomatopoeia' and of how poets use powerful vocabulary for effect. Children should be able to identify these features in the poetry that has been studied during the course of the first phase of this unit. Provide children with copies of the chosen narrative poem or display an enlarged copy on screen or on the board. Explain that they are to read the poem and fill in the chart on the photocopiable page 'Poetic devices' (version 1 or 2).

Assessment opportunity
Children working at levels 4-5 will work independently to identify any poetic devices, marking them on version 2 of the photocopiable page, giving examples and describing their effects. Children working at levels 2-3 should use version 1 of the photocopiable page and find one example of each poetic device listed in the chart. Draw out and deepen children's responses orally by asking them to describe how the poem makes them feel, to explore how the characters in the poem feel and act, and to identify any striking images or use of language, giving reasons and evidence from the poems.

Assessment evidence
Children working at levels 2-3 may identify one example of each of the poetic devices from the photocopiable page. Children working at levels 4-5 identify metaphors, similes, rhythm and rhyme, and are aware of how the use of repetition builds tension. Children's written and oral responses will provide evidence for Reading AF5.

Next steps
Support: For those children who need extra help in recognising metaphor and simile, provide other poems and ask them to find comparisons that use 'like/as' and those that do not.
Extension: Invite children to sit in the hot seat in the role of one of the characters in the poem.

Key aspects of learning
Evaluation: Children will present information orally, through drama and in writing. They will discuss success criteria, give feedback to others and judge the effectiveness of their own work.
Self-awareness: Children will discuss and reflect on their personal responses to the poems.
Communication: Children will develop their skills to reflect critically on what they have seen and read. They will develop their ability to present a poem orally and reflect critically on their own and others' work.

POETRY

Phase ② First person

Learning outcomes

- Children use their understanding of characters, language and plot to write in the first person.
- Children can reflect on how working in role helps to explore some of the complex issues within a poem.

Success criteria

- I can record opinions or thoughts about events in the poem in a first-person diary account.
- I can work in role to infer or deduce ideas about character.

Setting the context

Before running this assessment activity, ensure children have read and are familiar with the poem 'The Highwayman' by Alfred Noyes. Ask the children to work with a partner in groups of four or six children. Provide the group with a set of character cards from the photocopiable page 'Character cards'. Ask the pairs of children to pick one character card and devise between three and six questions they would like to ask the character on their card. Children working at levels 4-5 devise up to six questions, while children working at levels 2-3 devise three questions. As a class, choose children to sit in the hot seat as a character. Those who devised questions for that character should interrogate the hot-seated individual about their role and feelings in the poem's story. Invite the children to write a diary entry in the role of one of the characters using the first person.

Assessment opportunity

This activity provides the opportunity to evaluate children's abilities to work collaboratively, to empathise with characters and to make inferences and deductions to explore complex issues in a poem.

Assessment evidence

Children working at levels 2-3 will be able to write a straightforward recount of the events. Children working at levels 4-5 maintain viewpoint and demonstrate empathy with the character by describing emotions and feelings. Use children's oral responses and references to the text, along with your notes made during the role-play activities to provide evidence against Reading AF3, AF6 and AF7. Children's written diary responses will provide evidence for Writing AF1 and AF7.

Next steps

Support: For children who struggled to empathise with characters and write in role, ask pairs of children to role play a conversation between two characters from the poem.

Extension: Invite children to write another diary entry for a different character and compare how similar and different the entries are for both characters.

Key aspects of learning

Evaluation: Children will present information orally, through drama and in writing. They will discuss success criteria, give feedback to others and judge the effectiveness of their own work.

Self awareness: Children will discuss and reflect on their personal responses to the poems.

Enquiry: Children will investigate an older narrative poem, seeking the answers to their own and others' questions. They will engage in drama and discussion and then plan and present their own version orally and visually.

Phase ③ Group performance

Learning outcome
Children demonstrate that they can work as a member of a group to plan, perform and evaluate a choral performance of a poem.

Success criteria
- I can understand different ways to take the lead and support others in the group.
- I can evaluate my own work according to agreed criteria.

Setting the context
This assessment should be carried out after the children have created a group presentation of their chosen narrative poem. They should have drawn up a list of success criteria for reference. Briefly, recap the stages undertaken to create the presentations during the course of this unit. Invite each group to perform or show their presentation to the other children in the class. Working in pairs, ask the other children to make notes to evaluate each group's performance using the success criteria. Ask the pairs to give oral feedback to the groups and summarise their evaluations by saying what two things went well and what aspect the group could develop further.

Assessment opportunity
Observe children's performances and make notes against the class list in order to assess children's abilities to collaborate in groups. Pairs of children's notes and oral feedback can be used to evaluate the groups' performances. Invite groups to respond to the pairs' suggestions about aspects they could develop and improve.

Assessment evidence
Make judgements about children's peer evaluations against your own observations. Use children's presentations, written and oral feedback and notes made against the class list to provide evidence against Reading AF7.

Next steps
Support: Encourage children to use the evaluations to develop and refine their group presentations.
Extension: Encourage children to read and select other narrative poems they think are suitable for a choral performance.

Key aspects of learning
Enquiry: Children will investigate an older narrative poem, seeking the answers to their own and others' questions. They will engage in drama and discussion and then plan and present their own versions orally and visually.
Evaluation: Children will present information orally, through drama and in writing. They will discuss success criteria, give feedback to others and judge the effectiveness of their own work.
Self-awareness: Children will discuss and reflect on their personal responses to the poems.
Communication: Children will develop their skills to reflect critically on what they have seen and read. They will develop their ability to present a poem orally and reflect critically on their own and others' work.

Periodic assessment

POETRY

Reading

Learning outcome
Children understand the differences between literal and figurative language and can use the text to explain the effects of imagery in a poem.

Success criteria
- I can identify the structure of narrative poetry.
- I can identify the characteristics of a narrative poem.

Setting the context
Review the poetry read during the work on this unit and ask children to comment on which poems they preferred, with reasons for their choices. Encourage them to use the terms they have learned to describe why they like particular poems, such as figurative language, imagery, rhyme, metaphor and simile. Make notes of oral responses.

Assessment opportunity
Children work independently using the interactive activity 'Poetry 2 Reading assessment'. They answer a series of questions to identify a variety of characteristics of narrative poetry.

Assessment evidence
Children working at levels 4–5 will score highly on the interactive activity. At The children's completed interactive activity and your notes made on their oral responses can be used to provide judgements against Reading AF4.

Writing

Learning outcomes
- Children demonstrate that they are able to evaluate and improve their performance in the light of comments from others.
- Children can record their own evaluations of work and performance.

Success criteria
- I can evaluate my own work according to agreed criteria.
- I can identify key moments in the narrative.

Setting the context
Ensure children have read, analysed and performed poems. Review the work that has been completed during the course of Unit 2 and discuss individual children's achievements with them. Ask children to suggest what they found difficult about the work in the unit and what they found easy to accomplish. Remind children about their evaluations of the group performances of a narrative poem studied in the course of the unit. Invite them to write a journal entry to describe their own group's performance, the evaluations made by others and the effects of any steps they took to improve the performance in the light of those evaluations.

Assessment opportunity
This activity provides an opportunity to assess children's abilities to evaluate their own part in the group performance of a narrative poem. Encourage children to refer to the text of the poem to illustrate their group's successes and areas to refine.

Assessment evidence
Children working at levels 2–3 will write a straightforward recount of their group presentation and evaluative comments. Children at levels 4–5 will include steps they took to improve, with comments about their effectiveness and reasons for this. At all levels, the children's completed journal entries can be used to provide judgements against Writing AF2.

SCHOLASTIC

Character cards

■ Cut out the character cards. Think of questions to ask the characters.

## The Highwayman	## Tim, the ostler
## Bess, the landlord's daughter	## A soldier

POETRY
UNIT 3 Performance poetry

Learning objectives

Speak and listen for a wide range of purposes in different contexts

Strand 4 Drama
- Use and recognise the impact of theatrical effects in drama.

Read and write for a range of purposes on paper and on screen

Strand 7 Understanding and interpreting texts
- Infer writers' perspectives from what is written and from what is implied.
- Explore how writers use language for comic and dramatic effects.

Strand 8 Engaging with and responding to texts
- Compare the usefulness of techniques such as visualisation, prediction and empathy in exploring the meaning of texts.
- Compare how a common theme is presented in poetry, prose and other media.

Strand 9 Creating and shaping texts
- Reflect independently and critically on their own writing and edit and improve it.
- Adapt non-narrative forms and styles to write fiction or factual texts, including poems.

Strand 12 Presentation
- Adapt handwriting for specific purposes, for example printing, use of italics.
- Use a range of ICT programs to present texts, making informed choices about which electronic tools to use for different purposes.

Key aspects of learning

Enquiry
- Children will investigate a poem, seeking the answers to their own and others' questions. They will engage in drama and discussion and then plan and present their own version orally and visually.

Information processing
- Children will identify relevant information from a range of sources and use this as a basis for a choral performance of their own version of the poem.

Evaluation
- Children will present information orally, through drama and in writing. They will discuss success criteria, give feedback to others and judge the effectiveness of their own work.

Self-awareness
- Children will discuss and reflect on their personal responses to the poems.

Communication
- Children will develop their skills to reflect critically on what they have seen and read. They will develop their ability to present a poem orally and reflect critically on their own and others' work.

Assessment focuses

Reading
AF5 *(explain and comment on writers' use of language, including grammatical and literary features at word and sentence level).*

Writing
AF2 *(produce texts which are appropriate to task, reader and purpose).*
AF7 *(select appropriate and effective vocabulary).*

Speaking and listening
Drama (identify qualities of others' performance; sustain a role).

Resources

Periodic assessment
Photocopiable page, 'Poetry 3 Reading assessment text'
Photocopiable page, 'Poetry 3 Writing assessment'
Recommended texts
Performance poems by poets such as Wes McGee, Michael Rosen, Roger McGough and Tony Mitton

Unit 3 🔲 Performance poetry

Learning outcomes	Assessment opportunity and evidence	Assessment focuses (AFs)		Success criteria
		Level 2	Level 3	
Phase ① activity page 169				
Features of performance poetry Children can identify key features of performance poetry.	• Supported group activity where children draw up a list of criteria for performance poetry and choose a poem that meets the criteria. • Children's written and oral responses and notes against the class list.	**Reading AF5** • Some effective language choices noted. • Some familiar patterns of language identified.	**Reading AF5** • A few basic features of writer's use of language identified, but with little or no comment.	I can identify the key features of poems that make good performance poetry.
Phase ② activity page 170				
Performance techniques Children can write poems to reflect the identified techniques of performance poetry.	• Paired activity where children evaluate each other's and their own performance poems against a checklist of criteria. • Children's oral responses and notes made against the class list.	**Writing AF2** • Some basic purpose established. • Some appropriate features of the given form used. • Some attempts to adopt appropriate style.	**Writing AF2** • Purpose established at a general level. • Main features of selected form sometimes signalled to the reader. • Some attempts at appropriate style, with attention to reader.	I can write my own performance poem using identified techniques.

Learning outcomes	Assessment opportunity and evidence	Assessment focuses (AFs)		Success criteria
		Level 4	Level 5	
Phase ① activity page 169				
Features of performance poetry Children can identify key features of performance poetry.	• Independent activity where children draw up a list of criteria for performance poetry and choose a poem that meets the criteria. • Children's written and oral responses and notes against the class list.	**Reading AF5** • Some basic features of writer's use of language identified. • Simple comments on writer's choices.	**Reading AF5** • Various features of writer's use of language identified, with some explanation. • Comments show some awareness of the effect of writer's language choices.	I can identify the key features of poems that make good performance poetry.
Phase ② activity page 170				
Performance techniques Children can write poems to reflect the identified techniques of performance poetry.	• Paired activity where children evaluate each other's and their own performance poems against a checklist of criteria. • Children's oral responses and notes made against the class list.	**Writing AF2** • Main purpose of writing is clear but not always consistently maintained. • Main features of selected form are clear and appropriate to purpose. • Style generally appropriate to task, though awareness of reader not always sustained.	**Writing AF2** • Main purpose of writing is clear and consistently maintained. • Features of selected form clearly established with some adaptation to purpose. • Appropriate style clearly established to maintain reader's interest throughout.	I can write my own performance poem using identified techniques.

Phase ① Features of performance poetry

Learning outcome
Children can identify key features of performance poetry.

Success criteria
I can identify the key features of poems that make good performance poetry.

Setting the context
This assessment should be carried out once children have explored performance poetry and identified some key features, for example, repetitive lines, strong rhythm, onomatopoeia, verses and repeated refrains. Ask the children to work in small groups and draw up their own group's list of key features for choosing a poem to perform. Then provide them with a selection of poetry, for example, poems by poets such as Wes McGee, Michael Rosen, Roger McGough and Tony Mitton. Include some that would be unsuitable for a choral performance. Invite the children to read and compare the poems as a group and choose one that satisfies the criteria for performance.

Assessment opportunity
Children working at levels 4-5 will work independently to draw up a list of criteria and choose a poem. Children working at levels 2-3 should work in a group supported by an adult. As the group discuss the criteria and choose their poem, the supporting adult can make notes of individual contributions against the class list. Invite the groups to read their chosen poem aloud and explain the reasons for their choice.

Assessment evidence
Children working at levels 2-3 may identify success criteria in response to prompting. Children working at levels 4-5 will devise their own success criteria and use these to select an appropriate poem. Children's written and oral responses and notes made against the class list will provide evidence for Reading AF5.

Next steps
Support: For those children who struggled to choose a poem that met their criteria, provide a performance poem and ask them to annotate it to identify the features in their list of criteria.
Extension: Invite children to rehearse and polish the performance of their chosen poem.

Key aspects of learning
Information processing: Children will identify relevant information from a range of sources and use this as a basis for a choral performance of their own version of the poem.
Evaluation: Children will present information orally, through drama and in writing. They will discuss success criteria, give feedback to others and judge the effectiveness of their own work.
Self-awareness: Children will discuss and reflect on their personal responses to the poems.
Communication: Children will develop their skills to reflect critically on what they have seen and read. They will develop their ability to present a poem orally and reflect critically on their own and others' work.

POETRY

Phase ② Performance techniques

Learning outcome
Children can write poems to reflect the identified techniques of performance poetry.

Success criteria
I can write my own performance poem using identified techniques.

Setting the context
Run this assessment activity when the children have had the opportunity to decide on subject matter for their own performance poem and have written one using the ideas and models from a modelled writing activity. They should have referred to the checklist of criteria for performance poems from shared and group reading sessions in Phase 1 when writing their poems and should have allowed for opportunities to enable a performer to add expression, pace, and vary tone and volume. Invite the children to read their performance poem to a partner. Ask the partner to listen to the poem and, using the checklist of criteria, note which features their partner used in their writing. Ask them then to swap poems, to read each other's aloud and evaluate the effectiveness of their own poem.

Assessment opportunity
This activity provides the opportunity for children to evaluate each other's writing in pairs according to a list of criteria and to evaluate their own poem's effectiveness when read aloud by someone else. Invite the pairs to give oral feedback about their own and each other's performance poems.

Assessment evidence
At levels 2–3, children will make simple assessments of their own writing. At levels 4–5, children will include reasons for their assessments. Judge children's self-evaluations against your own observations made during the activity. Use children's oral responses and notes made against the class list to provide evidence against Writing AF2.

Next steps
Support: For children who struggle, revisit the poems read in shared and guided reading and annotate them according to the performance poem checklist.
Extension: Invite children to work in a group to evaluate another group's performance poems against the list of criteria.

Key aspects of learning
Evaluation: Children will present information orally, through drama and in writing. They will discuss success criteria, give feedback to others and judge the effectiveness of their own work.
Self-awareness: Children will discuss and reflect on their personal responses to the poems.
Communication: Children will develop their skills to reflect critically on what they have seen and read. They will develop their ability to present a poem orally and reflect critically on their own and others' work.

Periodic assessment

Reading

Learning outcomes
● Children can identify the key features of performance poetry.
● Children can apply varied tone-repeated patterns to a range of poems when performing.

Success criteria
I can identify the key features that make good performance poetry.

Setting the context
This assessment should be carried out after the children have completed Poetry Unit 3. Recap the work done on performance poetry. Briefly revisit the success criteria for performance poetry. Provide children with copies of the photocopiable page 'Poetry 3 Reading assessment text' which shows the poem, 'The Music Lesson' Rap by Clare Bevan. Arrange the children into groups of the same ability. Invite each group to discuss the poem, identify how best to perform it and annotate the poem to show where they might add sound effects or vary the tone to produce the best effect. Invite each group to perform the poem to the other children in the class. Working in pairs, ask the other children to make notes to evaluate each group's performance using the success criteria. Ask the pairs to give oral feedback to the groups and summarise their evaluations by saying which two things went well and which aspect the group could develop further.

Assessment opportunity
Observe children's performances and make notes against the class list in order to assess children's abilities to collaborate in groups. Children's notes and oral feedback can be used to evaluate the groups' performances. Invite groups to respond to the pairs' suggestions about aspects they could develop and improve.

Assessment evidence
Judge children's paired assessments against your own observations of the groups' performances and act accordingly. Use children's written and oral feedback and notes made against the class list to provide evidence against Reading AF5.

Periodic assessment

Writing

Learning outcomes

● Children can write poems to reflect the identified techniques of performance poetry.
● Children can review their own learning and evaluate it against clear criteria.

Success criteria

● I can write my own performance poem using identified features.
● I can review my own performance against agreed criteria.

Setting the context

This assessment should be carried out once children have completed Poetry Unit 3. Ensure children have had experience of reading and analysing performance poems in shared and guided reading. Children should have also had opportunities to draw up a checklist of the typical features of performance poetry and used these to write poems of their own both individually and collaboratively. Review the work that has been completed during the course of Unit 3 and discuss individual children's achievements with them. Ask them to suggest what they found difficult about the work in the unit and what they found easy to accomplish. Remind children about their evaluations of the group performances of a poem studied in the course of the unit. Encourage them to use the terms they have learnt to describe why they like particular poems, such as variation in tone, rhythm, onomatopoeia and rhyme. Make notes of oral responses against the class list. Invite children to complete the photocopiable page 'Poetry 3 Writing assessment'.

Assessment opportunity

Children work independently to complete their personal evaluation of a performance poem written and performed in the course of this unit. It could be a collaborative group poem or their own poem which has been independently written. This provides the opportunity to assess children's knowledge and understanding of the typical features of effective performance poetry.

Assessment evidence

Children working at levels 2–3 write a straightforward reason for their choice of poem based on the features it contains. Children working at levels 4–5 can elaborate on why certain features in the poem are effective. Use children's completed work from the unit, along with the photocopiable page and notes made against the class list of oral responses to provide judgements against Writing AF2 and AF7.

Poetry 3 Reading assessment text

The Music Lesson Rap

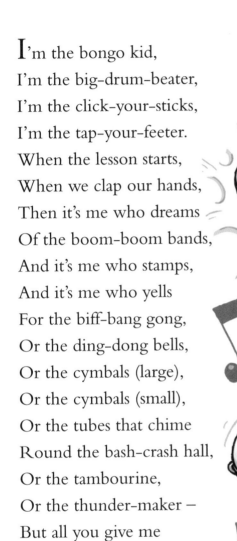

I'm the bongo kid,
I'm the big-drum-beater,
I'm the click-your-sticks,
I'm the tap-your-feeter.
When the lesson starts,
When we clap our hands,
Then it's me who dreams
Of the boom-boom bands,
And it's me who stamps,
And it's me who yells
For the biff-bang gong,
Or the ding-dong bells,
Or the cymbals (large),
Or the cymbals (small),
Or the tubes that chime
Round the bash-crash hall,
Or the tambourine,
Or the thunder-maker –
But all you give me
Is the sssh-sssh shaker!

Clare Bevan

Illustration © 2009, Simon Smith / Beehive Illustration.

Transitional assessment

Activity	Type	Level	Description
2.1	Reading comprehension	2	30-minute two-part test based on a narrative extract from *The Snow Lambs* by Debbie Gliori and the poem 'Weather at Work' by Jenny Morris
2.1	Shorter writing task	2	15 minutes; writing a report about different kinds of weather
2.1	Longer writing task	2	30 minutes; writing a recount based on personal experience of problem weather
3.1	Reading comprehension	3	30-minute two-part test based on narrative extracts from *The Sheep Pig* by Dick King-Smith and a non-fiction leaflet for a farm visitors' centre
3.1	Shorter writing task	3	15 minutes; writing an imaginative description of a special pet
3.1	Longer writing task	3	30 minutes; writing letter to persuade the teacher to take the class on a trip to a farm
4.1	Reading comprehension	4	40-minute two-part test based on extracts from *Street Child* by Berlie Doherty and an historical account about Dr Barnardo
4.1	Shorter writing task	4	20 minutes; writing a report on how a typical day in the classroom has changed since the 19th century
4.1	Longer writing task	4	40 minutes; writing imaginative recounts for Dr Barnardo's diary
5.1	Reading comprehension	5	40-minute two-part test based on non-fiction articles on healthy eating and two poems, 'My brother is making a protest about bread' by Michael Rosen and 'Oh, I wish I'd looked after me teeth' by Pam Ayres
5.1	Shorter writing task	5	20 minutes; writing a leaflet to explain 'Good Health Day'
5.1	Longer writing task	5	40 minutes; writing a cautionary tale about healthy eating

NB There are two transitional assessments provided for each level. Transitional tests and tasks 2.2, 3.2, 4.2 and 5.2 are not shown here. All tests and tasks are available on the CD-ROM.

Reading tests: instructions

There are two reading comprehension tests provided at each level (levels 2–5) on the CD-ROM. Each reading test is divided into two parts.

Administering the test
- Allow 30 minutes for both parts of the test at levels 2 and 3, and 40 minutes at levels 4 and 5.
- Children should work unaided.
- Do not read questions or words to them.

Equipment for each child:
- Pencil, eraser (or children may cross out mistakes).

Marking and levelling the children
- Mark the test using the Reading Mark Scheme provided on CD-ROM.
- Add together the marks from both parts of the reading tests (possible total of 30 marks).
- Use the levelling grid at the end of the Mark Scheme to level the test.
- When awarding an end-of-year Teacher Assessment Level, you will also need to consider a child's performance during Periodic and Day-to-Day Assessments. If a child has achieved a low level 3 or above in the transitional tests, it can be assumed that they have achieved AF1 at that level.

Writing tasks: instructions

There are two writing tasks provided at each level (levels 2–5) on the CD-ROM. Each writing task is divided into two parts: shorter and longer writing tasks.

Administering the tasks

Shorter writing task
Allow 15 minutes for each task at levels 2 and 3, and 20 minutes for each task at levels 4 and 5.

Longer writing task
Allow 30 minutes for each task, which could include 5 minutes' planning time at levels 2 and 3. Allow 40 minutes for each task, which could include 10 minutes' planning time at levels 4 and 5.
- Children should sit so that they cannot see each other's work.
- You may read the task to the children; do not explain the task or help them.
- The task may be administered to groups of children or to the whole class.
- Do not allow children to use dictionaries or word books.

Equipment for each child:
- Pencil, eraser (or children may cross out mistakes) and sheets of plain paper.

Introducing the writing tasks
Say to the children:
I am going to ask you to do some writing.
I will read the task to you, but I cannot help you with your ideas.
If you make a mistake, you should cross it out (or rub it out neatly) and write your word clearly.
Spell the words as best you can, building them up as you usually do.

Marking and levelling the children
- Mark each piece of writing separately using the Writing Mark Scheme, Table 1, provided on the CD-ROM.
- Double the marks gained for the longer Writing task and add this total to the mark gained for the shorter Writing task.
- Assess spelling and handwriting across both pieces of writing using Table 2, provided on the CD-ROM.
- Add the total gained from Table 1 to the total from Table 2.
- Use the grid at the end of the Mark Scheme to find a level for each child.